JOSEPH CONRAD
His Mind and Work

JOSEPH CONRAD
His Mind and Work

Kausar Equbal

SHIPRA

Rs. 400; US$ 20

ISBN: 978-81-7541-515-7

First Published in India in 2010

Joseph Conrad: His Mind and Work

Published by:

SHIPRA PUBLICATIONS

H.O.: LG-18-19, Pankaj Central Market, Patparganj,
I.P. Ext., Delhi 110092, Ph. 91-11-22235152, 22236152
Br. Off.: 115, Munish Plaza, 20, Ansari Road, Daryaganj,
New Delhi 110002; Ph. 91-11-65946453, 9810522367

Email: info@shiprapublications.com
Website: www.shiprapublications.com

Delicated to

My Parents

'Whose life is a pleasant memory,
Absence a silent grief,
Principles forever guiding,
vision always enlightening,
Blessings ever present.'

Preface

The facts of a writer's personal life are sometimes an unimportant element in the understanding of his work. With Conrad it is otherwise. His life and his works are so closely integrated that what passes for a story, for autobiography, for example 'A Personal Record' gives the flavour of a fiction. Joseph Conrad was capable of creation in the large sense, but he drew upon and returned again and again to the store of direct experience he had acquired in his dealings with fellowmen of almost everyrace and creed.

Conrad's output falls within the sphere of his writing which includes thirteen completed novels and seven volumes of short stories. They represent a body of work which shows the artist's avarice which seeks its treasure in the hearts of men and women. Unique in his experience, his vision, his blend of racial characteristics and natural gifts, Conrad stood alone in his own time. He wrote in his Note to 'The Nigger of the Narcissus': 'The artist...speaks to our capacity for delight and wonder, to the sense of mystery surrounding our lives; to our sense of pity, and beauty, and pain; to the latent feeling of fellowship with all creation'. These words are true of his own work. He was many things as a writer, but seldom less than an artist, and never so by intention.

In the present book I have tried to examine the evolution of the mind of the artist from personal to social awareness. The book, I hope so, will assist the reader to delve deep into the art of Conrad—a writer to whom one can return, at any time of life, with the assurance of refreshment.

I am grateful to Prof. S.N. Pandey of BHU and Prof. B.B. Singh of VKSU Ara for their constant guidance and blessings. I am thankful to my wife, Rahela Equbal and my sons, Sabeel and Nabeel for sparing me to accomplish this tedious work.They provided me every support and valuable opinions from time to time.

I put on record my appreciation and gratitude to Mr. D. Kumar of Shipra publications.

H-51/E
A.F.Enclave
Jamia Nagar
New Delhi-25

Dr Kausar Equbal

Contents

1

Introduction

Emile Legouis and Louis Cazamian say that Joseph Conrad is the most eminent symptom of what the new literary cosmopolitanism of the twentieth century might become if this vein is destined to grow broader:

> "No one before him had so definitely broken the light which binds the artistic handling of a given tongue to the exclusive possession of an intellectual nationality."[1]

Josef Teodor Konrad Korzeniowski was born in Russian occupied Poland in 1857. He died in England in August 1924. During his life-time he had been, at the age of five, a political exile with his patriot father, an orphan at the age of eleven, an exile from his country at Sixteen, an emigrant to England speaking only a few words of English at twenty, an ordinary sea man in the days of sail, a master in the British Mercantile marine, a traveller to the Far East, Africa and South Africa, a naturalized English man and a renowned novelist in English. Poland's loss was, in a sense, Britain's gain. Joseph Conrad chose England as his country and English as his medium and England was in the process to acquire one of her greatest novelists, one whose experience was international and ranged from the society of the polish aristocracy to that of seaman before the mast, whose life spanned the last years of the nineteenth century and the early years of this century, who knew Carlist gun-running in the Mediterranean, the quiet existence of British Villages, the lost lives of traders in the Jungles of Borneo, and the literary life of London as well as the life of its docks.

The language of his childhood and youth was polish; it remained that of his inner speech, except in moments of literary labour, when French stepped into its place. He was strongly influenced by the literature of France, and his technique is derived from that which was taught by our realists. English, first studied in books, then fully adopted by this mature personality, is the instrument of expression which his art employed in the process of explicit realisation.

And yet, thanks to an exceptional gift of assimilation, this instrument has the most extensive range. Joseph Conrad's vocabulary shows all the concrete wealth of the Anglo-Saxon stock; he displays, in some fields at least, a rare virtuosity in the use of technical terms, his knowledge of the things and words of the sea with which he is most intimately familiar-exceeds that of Rudyard Kipling. He knows, at need, how to seek effects in the ample dignity of Latin vocables. So glowing, luxuriant, and habitual is this delight in words, that it reveals, through its very development, a conscious apprenticeship of language, a manifest and all—comprehensive mastery; that abnormal something to which an English soil, the expert and complacent handl ing of linguistic resource seems to point. In fact Conrad's prose style at least during the early part of his career, would leave upon British ears an impression of slightly exaggerated sonorousness and rhythm.

His art is the most composite product. However essential may be the element of original initiative in his development, the form which he took up, either from instinctive choice or because he had experienced its appeal, had been created by others. It is the novel of adventure, whose new possibilities Stevensen and already Kipling were illustrating and he combined with it the objective of French naturalism. The movement and the method of his psychology, the attention he pays to the various points of view which cross and recross one another round each being, owe something to Henry James. Lastly a background of Slav sensibility,[2] and the spirit of Russian novelists, are portrayed in the special quality of his perception of the mysterious, and in his philosophy of life.

Emile Legouis comments: "This complex of influences is dominated by a temperament which turns it into a brilliant, rich and original alloy. Joseph Conrad was quite conscious of his manner. He has given a theory of it. This is the direct echo of his inevitable preferences; but one feels that it was encouraged as well by the doctrines of Maupassant and Flaubert. Art is self sufficient; the artist has no object but to fully transmit the impression of reality and the senses are the best or rather the only way open to this expression. Therefore, the novelist must draw from all the resources of the arts, whether of colour and shape or of sound. His work should have the bright hues of painting, the solidity of sculpture, the rhythm and harmony of music. He has fulfilled this programme to the letter, not with painstaking accuracy, but with sovereign ease of talent which when obeying rules is but following its own instinct. The wealth, the vigour, and the glow of his descriptions are second to none in literature. The scenes which he calls up are varied but their succession naturally finds a centre in the image of the sea. It's from the deck of the ship that we witness the ocean, the ship-board dramas, distant shores, the landscapes and manners of Oceania, of Asia, of America, and of those English sea ports where the liners find their way back, make up an intensely vivid show, forces itself upon our view like sticking, almost haunting decor".[3]

Conrad believed that the style of a novel must strenuously aspire to the plasticity of sculpture, to the colour of painting, and to the magic suggestiveness of music which is the art of arts. He was quite conscious of his manner, and has a theory of it. This is the direct echo of his inevitable preference. But one feels that it was encouraged as well by the doctrines of Maupassant and Flaubert. Conrad is rightly a stylist, broadly speaking, an artificer of splendid periods, an evoker of atmosphere, a translator of concrete phenomena into living words. His prose is rich, glowing, atmospheric, eloquent and superb. His prose style is in reality the translation of thoughts, feelings, and perceptions into words with the minimum loss of intensity. His is a style of extreme flexibility and interest. His style has a rich descriptive power. He can describe colourfully and vividly as in Soho in 'The Secret Agent', luxuriant jungle-scene, sunrise and all. Similarly, the interrupted voyage of Patna across the Arabian Sea has amazing descriptions:

"A marvellous stillness pervaded the world, and the stars, together with the serenity of their rays seemed to shed upon the earth the assurance of everlasting security. The young moon recurved, and shining low in the west, was like a slender shaving thrown up from a bar of gold, and the Arabian Sea, smooth and cool to the eye like a sheet of ice, extended its perfect level to the perfect circle of a dark horizon. The propeller turned without a check, as though its beat had been part of the scheme of a safe universe; and on each side of the Patna two deep folds of water, permanent and sombre on the unwrinkled shimmer, enclosed within their straight and diverging ridges a few white swirls of foam bursting in a low hiss, a few wavelets, a few ripples, a few undulations that, left behind, agitated the surface of the sea for an instant after the passage of the ship, subsided splashing gently, calmed down at last into the circular stillness of water and sky with the black speck of the moving hull remaining everlastingly in its centre.

A draught of air, fanned from forward by the speed of the ships passed steadily through the long gloom between the high bulwarks, swept over the rows of prone bodies; a few dim flames in globe-lamps were hung short here and there under the ridge poles, and in the blurred circles of light thrown down and trembling slightly to the unceasing vibration of the ship appeared a chin upturned, two closed eyelids, a dark hand with silver rings, a meagre limb draped in a torn covering, a head bent back, a naked foot, a throat bared and stretched as if offering itself to the knife. The well-to-do had made for their families shelters with heavy boxes and dusty mats; the poor reposed side by side with all they had on earth tied up in a rag under their heads; the lone old man slept, with drawn-up legs, upon their prayer-carpets, with their hands over their ears and one elbow on each side of the face; a father, his shoulders up and his knees under his forehead, dozed dejectedly by a boy who slept on his back with tousled hair and one arm commandingly extended; a woman covered from head to foot, like a corpse, with a piece of white sheeting, had a naked child in the hollow of each arm; the Arab's belongings, piled right aft, made a heavy mound of broken outlines, with a cargo-lamp swung above and a great confusion of vague forms behind: gleams of paunchy brass pots, the foot-rest of a deck-chair, blades of spears, the straight scabbard of an old sword leaving against a heap of pillows, the spout of a tin coffee-pat. The patent log on the taffrail periodically rang a single tinkling stroke for every mile traversed on an errand of faith. Above the mass of sleepers a faint and patient sigh at times floated, the exhalation of a troubled dream; and short metallic clangs bursting out suddenly in the depths of the ship, the harsh scrape of a shovel, the violent slam of a furnace door, exploded brutally, as if the men handling the mysterious things below had their breasts full of fierce anger: while the slim high hull of the steamer went on evenly ahead, without a sway of her bare masts, cleaving continuously the great calm of the waters under the inaccessible serenity of the sky.

Jim paced athwart, and his footsteps in the vast silence were loud to his own ears, as if echoed by the watchful stars: his eyes roaming about the line of the horizon, seemed to gaze hungrily into the unattainable, and did not see the shadow of the coming event."[4]

The tone of Conrad's prose is sometimes rhetorical. The rhetorical poet in Conrad never runs away with the novelist as it does in Thomas

Hardy. Yet Hardy's definition of his own artistic aim exactly fits that of Conrad to intensify the expression of things, so that the heart and inner meaning is vividly visible. But where Hardy boldly states Conrad evokes and suggests.

His tone of prose is conversational often. In 'Nostromo,' for example, he counterbalances the grandness of conception by a casual conversational manner which helps immensely in assuring the reader of the truth of the events described. Later, when 'Chance' is written, Conrad maintains the suggestion of the truth of the extraordinary situations by an extreme freedom of the conversational tone. This tone used as a device for persuading the reader that a story was nothing but the truth was less difficult stylistic achievement for Conrad than the adaptation of the style to the speech of simple, uneducated men and such characters as he used for a satirical purpose like Mr. and Mrs. Fyne in "Chance". Some of the funniest, and, in their way, the truest effects ever achieved in fiction are due to Conrad's amazing use of his adopted language to recreate the individualities of plain sea-men. Could anything be better than the conversations between Captain Mac Whirr and Mr. Jukes in Typhoon? In his novels and stories about the sea life, his humour is the richest. Let us enjoy the beautiful conversation between Mac Whirr and Jukes:

> "She (Nan-Shan) had come out on a British register, but after some-time Mrs. Sigg judged it expedient to transfer her to the Siamese flag.

At the news of the contemplated transfer Jukes grew restless, as if under a sense of personal affront. He went about grumbling to himself and uttering short scornful laughs. "Fancy having a ridiculous Noah's Ark elephant in the insight of one's ship", he said once at the engine-room door. "Dash me if I can stand it. I'll throw up the billet. Don't make you sick, Mr. Rout?"

The first morning the new flag floated over the stern of the Nan-Shan, (Chief Mate) Jukes stood looking at it bitterly from the bridge. He struggled with his feelings for a while, and then remarked, "Queer flag for a man to sail under, sir."

"What's the matter with the flag?" inquired Captain Mac Whirr. "Seems all right to me.'' And he walked across the end of the bridge to have a good look.

"Well, it looks queer to me", bursts out Jukes, greatly exasperated, and flung off the bridge. Captain Mac Whirr was amazed at these manners. After a while the stepped quietly into the chart-room, and opened his International Signal Code-book at the plate where the flags of all the nations are correctly figured in gaudy rows. He ran his finger over them, and when he came to Sian he contemplated with great attention the red field and the white elephant. Nothing could be more simple; but to make sure he brought the book out on the bridge for the purpose of comparing the coloured drawing with the real thing at the flagstaff astern. When next Jukes, who was carrying on the duty that day with a sort of suppressed fierceness, happened on the bridge, his commander observed:

> "There is nothing amiss with that flag". "Isn't there? mumbled Jukes, falling on his knees before a deck-locker and jerking there form viciously a spare lead-line.

"No, I looked up the book. Length twice the breath and the elephant exactly in the middle. I thought the people ashore would know how to make the local flag. Stands to reason. you were wrong, Jukes..."

"Well, Sir" began Jukes, getting up excitedly, "all I can say ..." He fumbled for the end of the coil of line with trembling hands. "That' s all right." Captain Mac Wirr soothed him, sitting heavily on a little canvas folding stool he greatly affected. "All you have to do is to take care they don't hoist the elephant upside-down before they get quite used to it." Jukes flung the new lead-line over on the fore-deck with a loud. "Here you are, bosun—don't forget to wet it thoroughly," and turned with immense resolution towards his commander; but Captain Mac Whirr spread his elbows on the bridge-rail comfortably.

"Because it would be, I suppose, understood as a signal of distress", he went on. "What do you think? That elephant there, I take it, stands for something in the nature of the Union Jack in the flag..."

"Does it!" Yelled Jukes, so that every head on the Nan-Shan's decks looked towards the bridge. Then he sighed, and with sudden resignation: "It would certainly be a dam distressful sight", he said, meekly."[5]

In the use of the English language, Conrad, originally a man from Poland, exhibited remarkable skill, and put many English authors to rout and shame. He cultivated the prose style of a lyric poet:

> "It is only that the moods of the sea, dawn in the tropical jungle, passionate love and bare heroism made the spirit of lyric poetry pulse in his prose, but his vision apprehends things with such imaginative energy that the spirit of poetry is never long absent."[6]

His prose bears close affinity to the prose of De Quincey and Ruskin. He could be master of English prose comparable in felicity of language and sweep of eloquence with the ornate prose writers of English language like Ruskin and Newman.

According to Walter Allen in 'The English Novel' Conrad's prose is always heightened, heightened to a degree much above what is normal in English. It is essentially eloquent, a prose of peroration, to the total effect of which everything is subdued: choice of words, rhythms, balance of clauses, length of sentences and culmination of paragraphs. Conard employed a few words: 'exotic', 'enigmatic', 'inscrutable' quite frequently in his writings. He wrung the maximum effect from the use of words. He employed rhythm and alliteration and achieved a prose style akin to poetry. He introduced a prose which was equally noble in its sonorous cadence, equally sure but when he wrote below his best, he became over ornamental, self conscious and artificial. He then entered into monotonies and repetitions trying to give the impression of colour and vigour which could not be possible in an artificial style. But with all these blemishes, his prose style is magnificent and can serve a good model for those who seek to fly on the wings of imagination to places remote and exotic and enjoy the sin of the seas and tropical forests.

His approach to language is poetical and he is aware of the magical potency of words. But Conrad's complex, contradictory nature baffles Polish critics who cannot separate Conrad—the pole—from Conrad the English novelist. Zabierowski's account of the continuing debate on the subject is fairly thorough and balanced. If it appears redundant, it is mainly because the same 'Polish' problems tend to be magnified, at times out of all proportion, by the critics in Poland. Thus, for example, Prince Roman, a minor piece in Conrad's novelistic cannon receives a great deal of attention primarily because of its theme rather than its intrinsic artistic merit. Polish critics harp on the duality of Conrad's nature, occasionally drawing sweeping conclusions about his philosophical outlook. To some of them, Conrad is no less than a romantic, a poet-prophet. Indeed, it is not too difficult to find some prophetic statements in Conrad's fiction, essays and correspondence. But again in their ardent desire to depict Conrad as a modern Krasinski.

Polish critics tend to exaggerate Conrad's art of presaging the future."[7]

Now let us see how Conrad counterbalances the grandness of conception by a casual conversational manner in his novel 'Nostromo'.

Arnold Kettle, professor of literature at the Open University, Milton Keynes, says:

> I will give one example of method of 'Nostromo', a passage following a scene of great intimacy between Antonia, the daughter of the idealist liberal leader, and Decoud, the skeptical unprincipled Europeanised dilettante, who is love in with her. It is late evening and they are standing in the window of Antonia's house. "She did not answer. She seemed tired. They landed side by side of the little balcony, very friendly, having exhausted politics, giving themselves up to the silent feeling of their nearness in one of those profound pauses that fall upon the rhythm of passion. Towards the plaza end of the street the glowing coals in the brazeros of the market women cooking their evening meal gleamed red along the edge of the pavement. A man appeared without a sound in the light of a street lamp, showing the coloured inverted triangle of his bordered poncho, square on his shoulders, hanging to a point below his knees. From the harbour end of the Calle a horseman walked his soft-stepping mount, gleaming silver grey abreast each lamp under the dark shape of the rider. 'Behold the illustrious Capataz de Cargadores', said Decoud gently, 'coming in all his splendour after his work is done..."[8]

Here we find several essentials of Conrad's method. The personal relationship, intimately yet objectively suggested, is placed, by the immediate evocation of the whole Plaza, securely within a larger social relationship, the private world related at once to the public world. The glowing coals, with their suggestion of after-passion, are at the same time surface objective, adding to the visual reality of the scene and an atmospherically valuable, a kind of bridge between the two worlds. The market women and the man in his poncho are not merely picturesque, they fill out involuntarily the social picture; and they give a warmth and significance to the politics that Antonia and Decoud have been discussing. And then, all within five sentences, the next character is on the scene: Nostromo, heralded by his conventional epithet "illustrious". And, already the image most often associated with Nostromo has appeared, silver. Silver-grey is his horse in the moonlight, gleaming like the silver buttons which he has magnificently ripped off his tunic to give to his admirer Morenita, and like the treasure of the San tome mine that will destroy him: all leading onward to the last sentence of the book when the name Nostromo, the dead captive of the mine, has been cried out across the sea by his lover:

> "In that true cry of undying passion that seemed to ring around from punta Mala to Azuera and away to the bright line of the horizon, overhung by a big

> white cloud shining like a mass of solid silver. the genius of the magnificent Capataz de Cargadoers dominated the dark gulf containing his conquests of treasure and love".[9]

Arnold Kettle says, "Even more remarkable, however, than the technical achievement is the moral honesty and political insight which Conrad brings to his masterpieces:[10]

> "What is wanted here is law, good faith, order, security", says Charles Gould, the owner of the silver mine. "Anyone can declaim about these things, but I pin my faith to material interests. Only let the material interests once get a firm footing, and they are bound to impose the conditions on which alone they can continue to exist."[11]

Again we find the following: "As against the mob the railway defended its property, but politically the railway was neutral."[12]

what a wealth of observation and understanding has gone to create such insights. The inadequacy of liberalism is most poignantly expressed in:

> "The feeling of pity for those men (the liberals), putting their trust into words of some sort, while murder and rapine stalked over the land..."[13]

And nearly all the liberals are shown as totally incapable of meeting the moment of danger.

A messenger from Hernandez, the notorious bandit, asks Charles Gould:

> "Has not the master of the mine any message to send to Hernandez, the master of the campo?" The truth of the comparison struck Charles Gould heavily. In his determined purpose he held the mine, and the indomitable bandit held the campo by some precarious tenure. They were equals before the lawlessness of the land. It was impossible to disentangle one's activity from its debasing contacts. A close meshed net of crime and corruption lay upon the whole country..."[14]

We are tempted to quote passages which show Conrad's consciously formulated understanding of the social situation he is recording; but the real test of a novel lies, of course, in its ability to convey artistically that understanding and for such a test the abstracted quotation is inadequate.

Mrs. Gould's disillusionment with effects of material interests is almost complete when Dr. Monygham says:

> "There is no peace and no rest in the development of material interests. They have their law and their justice. But it is founded on expediency and is inhuman; it is without rectitude, without the continuity and force that can be

> found only in a moral principle. Mrs. Gould, the time approaches when all the Gould concession stands for shall weigh as heavily upon the people as the barbarism, cruelty and misrule of a few years back."[15]

At the close of the novel her husband must leave her, at a moment when she needs help and consolation, because there is labour unrest in the mine. The workers are disillusioned too. And Mrs. Gould in her sad wisdom reflects:

> "It had come into her mind that for life to be large and full, it must contain the care of the past and of the future in every passing moment of the present."[16]

The tragedy of "Nostromo" is that he has none of this sense at all. He has no roots, he is an expatriate Italian. His great power and influence over the workers is exerted arbitrarily; he lives only for reputation. And when this is taken from him (by the failure of the liberal-capitalist alliance, which he has supported from no principle) he falls a prey immediately to the power and temptation of the silver of the mine. Thus Nostromo, though a 'natural' leader of the people and sharing their deepest hopes and aspirations as well as their fears and superstitions, is useless as a leader because he is without principle. He is a careerist.

But if Nostromo does not understand the point of Mrs. Gould's reflection, Conrad does; and it is in his profound comprehension that the greatness of the book ultimately lies. For it succeeds most wonderfully in capturing the truth of social movement. Engels once wrote:

> "History makes itself in such a way that the final result always arises from conflicts between many individual wills, of which each again has been made what it is by a host of particular conditions of life. Thus there are innumerable intersecting forces, an infinite series of parallelograms of forces which give rise to one resultant—the historical event. This again may itself be viewed as the product of a power which, taken as a whole, works unconsciously and without volition. For what each individual wills is obstructed by everyone else and what emerges is something that no one willed."[17]

It is extremely improbable that Conrad had ever read Friedrich Engels but this process which Engels describes in terms of science is precisely the total effect of 'Nostromo', achieved in terms of art—nothing less than the presentation of society in motion, history in the making.

Arnold Kettle says: "Conrad succeeds moreover in the immensely difficult task of conveying the inner-relation between the individual and society, the one and the many".[18]

According to Kettle Conrad succeeds, in fact, in the enormously difficult task of revealing imaginatively that "every man is a piece of the continent, a part of the main" and his triumph is more remarkable because in his personal outlook he would seem to have been far from clarity. This is shown particularly in "Nostromo" in his inadequate attitude towards 'the mob' who never come to life as human beings. And it emerges most significantly in a certain mistiness, which buried deep in the language and symbolism of the book, does, we must admit, sometimes blur the stupendous realism of the achieved work of art. It is no easy to isolate this quality—the quality that Mr. E.M. Forster is trying to catch when he writes of the central chasm of his tremendous genius and suggests that perhaps, "he is misty in the middle as well as the edges, that the secret casket of his genius contains a vapour rather than a jewel".[19]

It is not found at the heart of 'Nostromo' anything like a vapour. On the contrary, the quality of imagery in the greater part of the book is well compared to a jewel. Yet there are moments in the novel when a sense of the cruel futility of things does seem to overcome Conrad. "The cruel futility of lives and deaths thrown away in the vain endeavour to attain an enduring solution of the problem".[20]

With this sense __and it impregnates the end of the novel: the enigmatic enquiry on Nostromo's face before he dies, the presentation of his death as in some romantic sense a triumph 'the greatest, the most enviable, the most sinister of all', the ambiguity of the word 'dominated' in the final sentence. We may associate the failure of Mrs. Gould (and Conrad) ever to define at all clearly the meaning of 'material interests.' This recurring phrase plays so essential a part in the moral pattern of the book that its precise significance cannot be ignored. This is Mrs. Gould's moral discovery in the novel, a discovery from which Conrad never really dissociates himself:

> "An immense desolation, the dread of her own continued life, descended upon the first lady of Sulaco. With a prophetic vision she saw herself surviving alone the degradation of her young ideal life, of love, of work—all alone in the Treasure House of the world. The profound, blind suffering expression of a painful dream settled on her face with its closed eyes. In the indistinct voice of an unlucky sleeper, lying passive in the grip of merciless nightmare, she stammered out aimlessly the words—'Material Interests."[20]

Objectively it is clear that "material interest" stands for imperialism. It is the whole process and consequences of imperialist exploitation, so richly and concretely and humanely illuminated throughout the length of the book, that Mrs. Gould is brought up against. Why should it matter then that Conrad does not use the word (we are not after all reading sociology)? It matters, I think because it is the failure to recognize in its full theoretical and moral significance the process of imperialism that leads to the element of mistiness in Nostromo. Since "material interest" is not given a precise correlative, it achieves a vague and uncontrolled one. The implication begins to creep in that something in the very nature of things, something beyond human control (yet never defined), is responsible for the tragedy of 'Nostromo'.

It is not, of course, the failure to use the word imperialism that matters but a measure of failure to achieve artistic correctness. The reason for the failure is, I believe, quite clearly explained in Conrad's own experience. A Polish aristocratic nationalist, realistic and unsentimental in his liberal sympathies and consequently forced into exile, it was his attachment to Britain, his adopted country, that seems to have clouded his objectivity.

There is a significant sentence in 'Heart of Darkness' in which a distinction is drawn between the British Empire and all other empires. Marlow, examining a map of the world, remarks that there is no artistic relevance to the statement so that it can be abstracted. He said that there was a vast amount of red-good to see at any time, because one knew, that some real work was done there. It was his loyalty to the British empire that prevented Conrad, despite the immense honesty of his observation, from coming to an objective understanding of imperialism as such, just as it was his position as an aristocratic nationalist that gave such poignancy to his presentation in "Nostromo" of Viola the Garibaldino, the austere and noble Italian democrat who fathers Nostromo. In this case, however, Conrad does achieve artistic objectivity, does succeed in mastering what must have been an almost overwhelming temptation to idealise. For the Garibaldino, though personally admirable, is presented as ultimately ineffective. His principles are out of date; he cannot cope with the world of the San Tome silver mine. And he kills Nostromo whom his daughters love.

It is interesting that two characters in 'Nostromo' to the presentation of whom a residue of idealism clings are Mrs. Gould and Nostromo himself—a woman and the worker. This idealism is, in fact, responsible for the element of mistiness in the novel. It will not be untrue to say that Conrad never fully came to terms of 'Nostromo' but that this great writer should have triumphantly achieved, against appalling odds his 'moral discovery'—that vital sense of society changing, developing, becoming; of men mastering with almost infinite difficulty, agony and error, the problems they have to master. There is always a danger that in 'explaining' with reference to his life and background a writer's qualities we degrade both the writer and ourselves. It is as an artist, not as a rather muddle-headed Polish émigré, that Conard is of value to us Nevertheless a passage from his description of his youth in 'A Personal Record' is particularly illuminating:

> "An impartial view of humanity in all its degrees of splendour and misery together with a special regard for the rights of the unprivileged of this earth, not on any mystic ground but on the ground of simple fellowship and honourable reciprocity of services, was the dominant characteristic of the mental and moral atmosphere of the houses which sheltered my hazardous childhood: matters of calm and deep conviction both lasting and consistent, and with either."

Dr. F.R., Leavis has said in his valuable pages on Conrad in 'The Great Tradition':

> "About his attitude towards women there is perceptible all the way through his literary career, something of the gallant, simple sailor."[21]

This seems to be completely true. Almost all of Conard's women are idealized and this idealization is a subtle form of escape from reality. This is one angle of mistiness; the other lies in the 'enigmatic' quality of the masses. Once again the background of Eastern Europe in the nineteenth century may be significant. There is much of Conrad himself in the dilemma of Razumov, the hero of "Under Western Eyes:"

> "Between the two he was done for. Between the drunkenness of the peasant incapable of action and the dream-intoxication of the idealist incapable of perceiving the reason of things and the true character of men."[22]

"The wonder indeed, not that there should be an unresolved element of haziness removed as far as possible from that humanitarianism that seems to be merely a matter of crazy nerves or of a morbid conscience."[23]

We begin to see at such moments how it was that Conrad, standing on the very brink of the individualist quagmire of mysticism and neurosis, would not permit himself to be drawn into the bog. Sometimes he seems almost overwhelmed by the difficulty of "appraising the exact shade of mere mortal man, with his many passions and his miserable ingenuity in error, always dazzled by the base glitter of mixed motives, everlastingly betrayed by a short-sighted wisdom."[24]

But he pulls back, always carefully dissociating himself from 'that humanitarianism that seems to be a matter of crazy nerves or of a morbid conscience, always avoiding the seductive hopelessness of Original Sin.

Joseph Conrad has no conscious, intellectualised solution for the problems of the society which in 'Nostromo' he depicts with so much truth and insight. And indeed it is foolish to talk glibly of the 'solution' offered by a work of art, the experience of the work of art is in itself a kind of solution, a synthesis, a discovery of the nature of the problem. But even on the level of immediate helpfulness this great novel holds its surprises. By a stroke of astonishing intuition, the only man who is present with the dying "Nostromo"—symbol to Conrad of the people, "in his mingled love and scorn of life and in the bewildered conviction of being betrayed, of dying betrayed he hardly knows by what or by whom,"[25] is none of the main characters of the novel whom we already know, but an obscure little workman, a 'small, frail, bloodthirsty hater of capitalists' who, personally unadmirable and presented ironically, yet speeds Nostromo to his death with the assurance that, "the rich must be fought with their own weapons."[26]

Conrad has no idealized hero; the weakness of nature everywhere asserts itself. In spite of the endeavours of the best, themselves fallible, ineradicable selfishness turns man into a wolf to a man. The son of political exile, the child of a nationality and a race long persecuted, reveals himself in the pressing suggestion of union, pity and solidarity which emanates from his work. This appeal lends it a glow of sympathy, and raises it above the level of fiction-pure and simple. But its most contagious idealism lies in the tragic and dreamy sense of the unfathomable unknown which we brush past at every moment and in that mystic spiritualization of the face of life or that of earth, which suddenly casts glamour of poetry over the outlines of the action or the landscape.

But Zydzislaw Najder writes in the research paper 'Conrad and Rousseau-Concepts of Man and Society':[27]

> "There is also in Conrad's work four factors which conflict with the conservative style of thought. Firstly, political problems are for him essentially normal problems; in this as in several other respects, he stands at the opposite pole of Carlyle. Secondly, he rejects the supremacy of the state, the government, all established official institutions, even the law, over traditional values and over individuals and their spiritual claims. Thirdly, the postulate of equality as a component of liberty—which evoked the strongest protests from the conservatives—is evidently acceptable to him. And, fourthly, his attitude to property is as scornful as any revolutionary's.

Passing from general categories of a style of thought to the concrete presentations of social reality in Conrad's work, we face the same puzzling dilemma: the author of "Nostromo" and "The Secret Agent" can hardly be described as a conservative; but how can we describe his political attitude, if not as conservative? Not only in the two novels mentioned, but also in, for instance, "The Mirror of The Sea" and "Autocracy and War", we can discern an acute consciousness of the need for fundamental social and political change, an awareness of widespread injustice and corruption and a strong disapproval of status quo. This conservative was an outspoken critic of contemporary bourgeois society and of a system which gives first place and free play to 'material interests.' It is remarkable that his criticism reminds us more of those romantic and feudal' critics of the capitalists who were so vocal at the beginning of the nineteenth century, than of contemporary radical attacks on the prevailing economic and social stratifications. But unlike those conservative critics of capitalism and industrialism, Conard was no apologist for the feudal system, which was also due for an essential change. How can one explain this dilemma? But how one account for the fact that when Conrad postulates change, evolution, reform, he does not start from the present, but from a point in the past, before the plague of material interests had spread and before other pernicious forces of the present had begun their work of corruption."[28]

"The answer is to be found in Conard's peculiar political background. It is a peculiar characteristic of nineteenth century Polish political thought that its dominant trends are the same progressive and traditionalist."[29]

Najder goes on commenting about Joseph Conrad in this manner:

> "All Polish thinkers had to be traditionalist, or even conservative, because they wanted to restore their partitioned country. The restoration of national independence was the principal bẻlief, the first point of the agenda, of everybody who did not acquiesce in Poland's annihilation. To accept the present as the basis for the change would have meant to resign from the national, to renounce the glories of the past. This conservative impulse was strengthened by a constant need to preserve remnants of the old order in the form of language, tradition and customs. But, despite everything, Poles remained in the vanguard of international radical movements throughout the nineteenth century, fighting on innumerable barricades, and supporting or even leading revolutionary movement in Italy, Hungry and France-including the ill-starred Paris Commune, in which the commander of the armed forces was Jaraslow Dabrowski, an old companion of Conrad's father and uncle in their underground work."[30]

It is difficult to define Conrad's politics because it reflects his own political confusion. Joseph Conrad passionately rejected autocracy and authoritarianism as contrary to all that he valued most in man. He was free from local, provincial or national prejudices. He was born in Poland and spent his early life on the sea. He became by choice a writer of English rather than French, which he considered useful and began to run into fiction the material acquired in his wanderings specially in the South Seas.

Conrad's stories are distinguished for certain qualities of narrative art, notably a tendency, somewhat like Meredith's and Henry James', to postpone the crisis and defeat expectation. The result is to concentrate the force of the situation in a total effect of explosive intensity. The feature of the short story has been adopted by the novelist, and in Conard's case with extraordinary success. Again, he deals with characters of a powerful and bizarre originality, tested by strange condition and extraordinary events. Above all, he handles scene with wonderful effect to create that significant and influential medium which we call atmosphere. 'Victory', in its slow arranging of circumstances and human forces, its prolonged tension and its final surprising and total catastrophe, is a typical example of Conard's in his longer work. "The Heart of Darkness" is a magnificent example of atmosphere determining the unity and total effect of the short story. The heavy tropical air of equatorial Africa broods like a miasma over the monstrous and uncouth works of nature, twisting humanity itself into similar forms of atrocious inhumanity.

Cazamian and Raymond Las Vergnas present Conrad in this manner:

> "The registering of lights, sounds, odours. and tastes is with Joseph Conrad's characters a constant, automatic activity, which none of the emotions of life can interrupt. The artist who has fixed so many sensations and found the most fitting words to express them, has contributed, along with Kipling, to broaden the descriptive range of the English language".[31]

References

1. Legouis and Cazamian; History of English Literature; Revised Ed. 1987; p. 1331.
2. According to Webster. (Encyclopaedia Edition) Lexican publications, INC New York, Revised Ed 1996, Slavs are members of a group of Eastern European Peoples, usually subdivided into Eastern Slavs (Great Russians, Ukranians and Byelorussians) Western Slavs (e.g. Poles, Moraviars, Czechs, Slovaks) and southern slaves (e.g. Serbs, Croats, Slovense and Bulgars).
3. *Ibid.*, p. 1932-33.
4. Conrad, Joseph, Lord Jim. Mayoor Paper books, Noida, India, 1987; p. 13-14.
5. Conrad, Joseph. Typhoon, Surjeet Publications, Kamlanagar, Delhi, Indian reprint, 1989; p. 9-11.
6. A.S. Collins, English Literature of the 20th Century; p. 21.
7. Gillon, Adom, "Conrad's Reception in Poland for the last Sixty years". The Macmillan Press Ltd. 1979. (A commemoration Volume; p. 212)
8. Conrad, Joseph, Nostromo, part II, Chap V, Surjeet publications, Delhi 1989. Arnold Kettle, An introduction to English Novel, B.I. Publication; Delhi.
9. *Ibid.,* Cho III, X III.
10. Kettle, Arnold, An Introduction to the English Novel, Part II: The twentieth Century. The First Quarter B.I. Publication, 1978; p. 67-68.
11. *Ibid.,* Part I. Ch VI.
12. *Ibid.*, Part III. Ch I.
13. *Ibid.*, Part III, Ch IV.
14. *Ibid.*, Part III, Ch III.
15. *Ibid.*, Part III, Ch XI.
16. *Ibid.*, Part III, Ch XI.
17. Letter to J. Block 21st September, 1890.
18. Kettle Arnold, An Introduction to English Novel II, 1978 (2nd Ed); p. 70.
19. *Op. cit,* p. 135.
20. *Ibid.,* Part III, Ch XI.
21. Leavis, F.R., 'The Great Tradition', Fellow of Downing college, Cambridge Chatto and windus, London. *op cit.*; p. 135.

22. Conard, Joseph, "Under Western Eyes", pub. 1953, part I, section II.
23. Conard, Joseph, "A Personal Record", Author's Note (1925 Ed); p. IX.
24. Conrad Joseph, "Under Western Eyes", Part Section II.
25. Conrad, Joseph, "Nostromo", Author's Note.
26. *Ibid.*, Part III, chapter XIII.
27. Najder is editor of Tworczose, Warsaw. He has taught both philosophy and English and Polish literature in America as well as Poland. His publication in English includes Conrad's Polish Background and Values and Evaluation. He has also worked on a biography.
28. Najder Zydzislaw, "Conrad and Rousseau" from Papers the 1974 International conference on Conrad, Macmillan; p. 87-88.
29. *Ibid.*, p. 13-14.
30. *Ibid.*, Conrad and Rousseau; p. 88.
31. Cazamian and Ramond Las Vergnas, History of English Literature, Revised edn. 1987, (book VIII), Macmillan India Ltd.; p. 1333.

2

Political Philosophy

Man's vision of life is conditioned by his environment, by his reading and experiences. So was the case with Conrad. As a child, he was lonely, a suffering soul. His parents died in most distressing circumstances. He was left orphan at the tender age of fifteen. He was often ill, and once narrowly escaped death. His was a miserable, lonely, suffering and suffocating life. All these circumstances made his vision of life gloomy and pessimistic. Mrs. Conrad has observed, "he was not a happy nature, and he often anticipated trouble long before it came."

Conrad's profound concern with problems of moral failure, of desertion, of betrayal, in a large part also sprang from guilt feelings about his own abandonment of Poland—Poland helpless under an alien tyranny. At sixteen he went off to France and the sea. No doubt, unconsciously, he was taking the first step towards the abandonment of the land for which his ancestors, indeed his own father and mother suffered a lot and died. The abandonment was made exactly eleven years later when he took up British citizenship. He developed a sense of guilt by this act which became the inspiration of much of his writing and, most clearly of all, Lord Jim's fatal jump to safety echoed the young Korzeniowski's flight from Poland.

Due to this act, an atmosphere of sombreness and pessimism broods over the novels of Conrad. His characters prove too feeble in their struggle against the forces of nature. "The heavy tropical air of equatorial Africa broods like a miasma over the monstrous and uncouth works of nature, twisting humanity itself into similar forms of atrocious inhumanity."[1] Gustav Morf said "Lord Jim is more than a novel, it is a confession", it is a psychoanalytical novel written before psychoanalysis was founded".[2] Life indeed in Conrad's books is a hostile force; how malignantly hostile nature could be, is most powerfully shown in "The Heart of Darkness", in which the evil power of the African jungle converts an idealist into a living Pagan deity fit for the savage tribes who worship him. In the battle against nature, many fail and Conrad's interest, as often with Browing, lies frequently in the failures, in analyzing the weakness of a man's character, and so does Shakespeare, he often fits a man against just those circumstances that are fatal to his weakness.

Conrad like Mathew Arnold emphasized the lonely aspects of human life. His characters are isolated, calling to each other across the void of everlasting separation, saying 'we live', as we dream alone. Like the 'Ancient Mariner' of Coleridge, he often felt:

> "Alone, alone, all, all alone,
> Alone on a wide, wide sea."

The world of illusion recovers all through his novels. Man in his view is a funny, deluded creature pursuing the phantoms of his brain ceaselessly which, however, lead him to his destruction often he refers to faith, hope, love, fear, pity, ambition, patriotism and all other affections and ideals, as if they were merely illusions.

The political issues raised in Conrad's fiction attracted scant notice during his lifetime. He was also gravely disappointed by lack of public response to "Autocracy and War," his longest piece of political journalism. But within the last thirty years Conrad as a political writer has been given a growing consideration. Still, the conceptual framework of his thought, the sources and implications of his fundamental ideas of man, society and historical process, and the relation of his beliefs to the main currents of European political philosophy has not been much explored. "Conrad's political convictions remain to a large extent insufficiently defined".[3]

In the thirties the label "conservative" was affixed to Conrad and it stuck. But Prof. Howe and Kettle wrote later on Conrad's "realistic presentation of social and political conflicts".[4] Conservative is an epithet still used automatically in characterising Conrad's views. Prof. Avrom Heishman was the first to place Conrad within what he calls "the Burke tradition". Indeed there are evident affinities between Conrad's and Burke's attitudes, but there are also serious differences between them in their conceptual framework. For instance, where Conrad writes about the nation and humanity, Burke has the state and society. In fact, in the understanding of the nation Burke is closer to Rousseau than to Conrad. "Moreover, to place Conrad within the Burke tradition, that is within the tradition of the thinker generally considered to have been the father of modern conservation, makes it rather awkward to account for, or even to point at those elements of Conrad's thought which do not belong to and indeed clash with this tradition."[5]

Rousseau is the only thinker with a similar scope of interests that Conrad knew. But, inspite of superficial resemblance, Conrad was even more radically opposed to and less influenced by Carlyle than Rousseau. Not that the comparison with Rousseau himself presents no difficulties. It is well-known that he was a man of split personality and that his writings, even his developed theories, abound in contradictions. He, the sentimentalist, disappears with hardly a trace in his social contract; his philosophy of the individual seems to conflict with his philosophy of the State. Rousseau appears twice in Conrad's work: in "A Personal Record", with reference to "The Confessions" and Emile, and in "Under Western Eyes" where a reference to 'the Social Contract' is made and where a movement of Jean-Jacques plays quite an important role—one exile watching another exile.

Commenting upon 'The Confession', Conrad ironically shrugs off Rousseau's thoroughness in justifying his own existence and calls him—also ironically I presume—"an artless moralist."[6] And indeed, to a writer so passionately concerned with the problems of moral responsibility, 'The Confessions' must have appeared as primarily an exercise in self-exculpation.

Conrad's gibe at confessions as a 'discredited form of literary activity' acquires a peculiar significance in view of his own frequent use of this very convention. His heroes quite often indulge in confessions of two different types. The first is a straight forward disclosure of a painful, or otherwise important experience, 'an opening of one's heart to a friend', as we have in 'The Lagoon', 'Karain', 'An Anarchis,' 'Jukes', later in 'Typhoon', 'Chance', and finally in 'The Shadow Line', which is sub-titled 'A Confession'. "The function of such concession is to unburden one's soul by communing with another person."[7]

The other type is an apologetic confession: its objective is not so much to communicate as to justify oneself. Chapters four to eleven of 'Lord Jim' 'Falk' and large parts of 'Under Western Eyes' contain, or are based on confessions of this kind. In fact in 'Under Western Eyes' we have also a third type of 'confession':

> 'Razumov's secret report to the Russian police, the scornful and conceited

> missive which this 'man of reason', driven by best intentions, composes under the benevolent effigy of Rousseau. He feels perfectly safe when he writes it on a solitary islet devoted to the philosopher who maintained that man is innately good and that democracy is an excellent system but suitable only to people who are sufficiently mature.

Different as their subjects are, Jim's confessions to Marlowe in the first part of the novel and Razumov' s confessions in his diary, have in common not only their self-exculpating purpose, but also the way in which the arguments are developed. Both Jim and Razumov point to the peculiarities of their respective situations, which make it nonsensical to demand from them a 'conventional' kind of behaviour. Both stress their good intentions and their reasonableness. In the early chapters of the novel, Jim explains away his desertion of the 'Patna' by arguing that to remain on-board was practically pointless and that he never intended to shirk his duty. Razumov's explanation of his betrayal of Haldin follows a different course; he uses historical, political, and philosophical arguments to support his decisions—but the essential argument is the same: he was tricked by the circumstances, he did the only sensible thing, and his motives were pure and nonegoistic. Thus, in both cases we encounter a characteristically Roussean type of self-justification by reference to the exceptionality of one's situation and personality, and to one's good intentions.

"In any case Conrad's ethic of fidelity and constraint of duty, honour and human solidarity, was directly opposed to that of Rousseau and was rooted in a fundamentally different concept of human nature."[8] Bertrand Russell was the first to comment that "Conrad's point of view was far from modern which has two philosophies—the one which sweeps aside all discipline as unnecessary; the other, which finds its fullest expression in totalitarianism, which thinks of discipline as essentially imposed from without. Conrad adhered to the older tradition that discipline should come from within. He despised indiscipline, and hated discipline that was merely external."[9]

"Man is born a coward", says the French Lieutenant in 'Lord Jim'. "It is a difficulty, Parblea! It would be too easy otherwise. But habit-habit-necessity-do you see? The eyes of others—Voila. One puts up with it."[10] The 'older tradition' voiced here goes far back to ancient Greece. Man is naturally, spontaneously, neither virtuous nor strong; he has to be educated to given examples to follow; he must work on himself, but cannot be morally self-reliant. To Aristotle's dictum, that

"Man outside society is either God or beast". Conrad adds in 'Heart of Darkness' that a man who wishes to be a God becomes inevitably a beast."[11] Kind emotions and good intentions have a limited ethical value: were not both Kurtz and Charles Gould men of good intentions. And though a man can rise to greatness, he cannot put a simple trust in himself because of his inherent frailty.

Characteristically, Conrad criticised the modern democratic or semi-democratic state on two counts. "Firstly with Rousseau who would agree with, for depersonalising and emasculating its citizens, for turning them into cogs of huge socio-economic machinery. And secondly, for achieving what Rousseau had demanded in getting rid of traditional bonds and institutions, for atomising the human community. So, the typical products of human society, as Conrad suggests are economic robots and moral anarchists."[12]

The world of illusion recurs all through Conrad's novels. Man in his view is a puny, deluded creature pursuing the phantoms of his brain ceaselessly which, however, lead him to his destruction. Often he refers to faith, hope, love, fear, pity, ambition, patriotism and all other affections and ideals, as if they were merely illusions.

"We live as we dream-alone,"[13] says Marlow; and Conrad is obsessed with this incapable, desolating condition of experience. Lord Jim, Emilia Gould, Nostromo, Lingard, Verloc, Captain Whalley, Heyst and Lena—all are alone in their struggle, all feel the tremendous fact of our isolation, of the indestructible loneliness that surrounds, envelops, clothes every human soul from the cradle to the grave, and perhaps, beyond... Gustav Marf says in 'The Polish Heritage of Joseph Conrad' that he was simply projecting his own fate as an expatriate. Actually, he remained very much a Pole—an alien at heart to the end of his days.

Certainly he was not rooted, like Hardly, in the English soil nor like Galsworthy in English Society. Almost all his heroes are like himself—outcasts, melancholy and aloof. This proves his pessimistic vision of life; he finds misery and gloom in life which is surrounded by evil forces in human life. Because of an atmosphere of darkness and gloom in his novels, he has been called a pessimist, but Conrad denies this charge. He said, a true pessimist feels that life is not worth living and that it would have been much better not to have been born at all. Even Thomas Hardy is a pessimist in this sense, but only in his last novel. His approach to life and its problems is not nihilistic, it is constructive. He suggests ways and means by which human suffering can be mitigated and the maximum of happiness assured. Man can only survive by endurance, courage, human solidarity and fidelity.

Fidelity to one's community or to oneself—a sense of one's duty to oneself and to society can go a long way to mitigate the hard lot of man. Fidelity implies sincerity, duty, integrity and solidarity; it is fidelity which binds man to man, assuages his withering sense of loneliness; and results in brave and noble achievement. Thus, his attitude towards life is realistic. He is quite aware of the sorrow and suffering of the wickedness and triviality of human life. He summarised the history of human beings in a sentence: "They were born, they suffered, and they died and yet it is a great tale." In another occasion he remarked: "It is very difficult to be wholly joyous or wholly sad on this earth". In 'A Personal Record', he observed: "The aim of creation cannot be ethical at all. I would fondly believe that the object is purely spectacular; a spectacle for awe, love, adoration, or hate, if you like, but in this view, and in this view alone never, for despair."[14] Though Conrad's attitude to life may be sometimes pessimistic, yet as Richard Curle points out, "his philosophy of character is always optimistic". His approach to life and its problems is not nihilistic, it is constructive. He suggests ways and means by which human suffering can be mitigated and the maximum of happiness assured.

Loyalty is the towering human virtue, and from it springs all other virtues. Conrad's writing may be seen as a fantasia on fidelity or exact performance of duty. One sentence from his preface to 'A Personal Record' proves it:

> "Those who read me know my conviction that the world, the temporal world, rests on a few very simple ideas; so simple that they must be as old as the hills. It rests notably amongst others, on the idea of fidelity. There are several characters in the novels of Conrad who have no qualities other than fidelity and courage."[15]

Nobility is the barrier man erects against nothingness, against corruption, against evil which is all about him, insidious, waiting to engulf him, and which is, in some sense within him unacknowledged. Man lives in hostile environment whether the sea or the tropical jungle—and fidelity alone can enable him to face this hostility. Fidelity results in solidarity which is the cardinal virtue on the high sea. But when the barrier of fidelity breaks down to man, when the evil without is acknowledged by the evil within, then the fidelity is submerged. This fidelity itself is Conrad's central theme of his novels.

Conrad was not a psychologist like Henry James, but he was certainly a moralist, emphasizing in his novels the principle of fidelity and preservation of human trust. Betrayal of trust and the distracting power of evil in human life seemed to him to be heinous sin to be condemned and deprecated in fierce language.

The ideal of fidelity is essentially the ideal of personal honour and loyalty to his fellowmen, and it runs through his work 'like a guiding thread of gold'. Conrad's principle of fidelity, human solidarity, his political standpoint, of his concepts of society, inevitably focuses on his political novels 'Lord Jim', 'Victory,' 'The Secret Sharer', 'Under Western Eyes' and in his essay 'Autocracy and war' and his attitude to things Russian. But it was his 'Under Western Eyes' which received most attention.

Zdzislaw Najder's comparison of Rousseau and Conrad elucidates Conrad's concepts of man and society with the principle of human solidarity, pointing to Conrad's "opposition obsession syndrome"[16] in relations to Rousseau's claim for individual uniqueness and the consequent need for freedom.

Conrad's ideas rest on fidelity (faithful performance of duty). Nothing stirred his admiration as profoundly as the keeping of faith between man and man. He who injured another (or even refrained from helping another) was in the terms of Conrad's philosophy, betraying the whole human brotherhood. Conrad was much concerned with the problem of evil, and he saw evil within man as well as in the environment in which he lived and had his being. Albert once wrote "like Hardy, Conrad had a profound sense of the tragedy of life but it did not lead him to a spirit of resentment or accusation. In man's struggle against hostile forces, in his display of loyalty, courage, and indurance, in the face of heavy odds, he saw the finest thing in human life. Yet, from the frequency with which he portrays men of faith and courage, human solidarity, determined to abide by their duty, it is easy to see that for Conrad these were the prime virtues."[17]

Conrad intricately poured in his works the principle of fidelity and faith between man and man stirred with the evil nature of human life. The principle of human solidarity can be said as the recurrent theme of his stories. 'Lord Jim' is one of the most important human documents in English literature. It is a tragedy not of an individual, but of the humanity itself at cross-roads. It has been often compared with 'Hamlet' of Shakespeare, because it presents the hero in his moments of indecision—when his capacity for decisive action is completely paralysed. Jim, the second officer on the ship Patna, betrayed the pilgrims while jumping from it for his own safety, at a time when the ship, of which he was in charge, was on the verge of sinking. It was an act of betrayal of trust, Jim later succeeds to grow out of his past failures only when he jumps into the trust, the love, the confidence of the people, only when he shares that conception of life includes all mankind. The history of Jim is the history of all human individuals. Conrad says that "each blade of grass has its spot on earth whence it draws its life, its strength; and so is man rooted to the land which he draws his faith together with his life. Man fails as long as he is an uprooted human individual, while he succeeds when he jumps into the love and confidence of the vast multitude of mankind".[18]

"The Secret Sharer" lands us in a different situation, reaches a new understanding of life. In this novel, a fugitive from justice is given refuge on the high seas by the narrator of the story, a ship's captain. The narrator acts instinctively upon the principle of fidelity. He feels immediately that there is a fellow creature bound inseparably to himself, and therefore to be protected from the thing in pursuit-man made justice. "In this story Conrad's idea of fidelity and human solidarity is powerfully projected, not by statement but in action."[19] So, the problem of human isolation always haunted Conrad. It is very difficult for a man to be relieved of his inner darkness to be lifted out of his loneliness and abject and morbid capitulation. He can be saved only if he responds to the claims of the outer life, only if he accepts the values of human solidarity.

In 'Nostromo' written in 1904, Conrad is generally concerned with man in society, but from different perspectives. Man is seen at different levels—political, economic, social, religious, military and personal. In his earlier works, his characters move in their own worlds of privacy and isolation, here they come out in the open and struggle to take their individual and independent positions in society. Conrad himself described 'Nostromo' as a story of "events flowing from the passions of men short-sighted in good and evil."[20] There is in 'Nostromo' an acute awareness of the contradictions in human nature. Conrad knew that men often pretend to what they are not, or deceive themselves about their real motives, or use for their own advantage the gullibility of others. Conrad often treated these with great scorn.

In" Victory" written in 1915—the last testament of Conrad—we are introduced to a human drama of great intensity and immensity. It is in a way the summing up of Conrad—the tempest of his career. 'Victory', if not the greatest, is the most firmly modelled and most bodily wrought. The theme of violence just under the surface is continued in 'Victory' which opens in the voice of an anonymous narrator—who soon disappears. The tale begins at a distance from the island paradise, the retreat where we see Baron Heyst, the hero sitting:

> "An island is but the top of a mountain ... his most frequent visitors were shadows, the shadows of clouds, relieving the monotony of the inanimate, brooding sunshine of the tropics. His nearest neighbour—I am speaking now of things showing some signs of animation—was an indolent volcano which smoked faintly all day with its head just about the northern horizon."[21]

The characters are drastically simplified, take on something of the quality of figures in a morality play, each represents a facet; a facet of experience, or a type of mind. But "all the characters at first exist in a fragmentary fashion drawn with a few obsessional traits; Schimberg garrulous teller of Vile tales, compulsive trader in the fears and miseries of mankind, had first appeared in 'Lord Jim', then in 'Falk', so he is himself a kind of spectre from earlier tales; and his famous fable d' note might be taken as an illustration of Schopenhauer's theory that to eat is the first and most primitive form of absorbing the world into the self."[22]

The tale is simply told; there is no narrator's perspective, there is neither irony, humour nor comments in the telling; the irony, humour and the comments such as they are, belong to Heyst. Conrad, throughout his long artistic career, has always been preoccupied with study of man in society of destiny in a world of strife and challenges. In spite of his surface scenticism, in spite of his realisation of the forced sense of isolation of the modern man, Conrad stands by the virtues of fidelity, courage, solidarity and disinterested human action. Axel Heyst, the hero of 'Victory', reached this realisation of human solidarity and love-purged by the fire of death.

In the eyes of Conrad, the position of an artist is more like that of a thinker or a scientist who tries to know the fundamentals of life. Of course, the thinker deals in ideas while the scientist deals in facts. According to Conrad, the artist, the thinker and the scientist—all prepare us for the challenges of life, for the risky or dangerous or uncertain enterprise of living. Conrad says that the thinker and the scientist speak authoritatively to their common sense, to their intelligence, to their desire of peace or to their desire of unrest; not seldom to their prejudices, sometimes to their fears, often to our egotism but always to their credulity; and their words are heard with reverence, for their concern is with the weighty matters; with the cultivation of their minds and the proper care of their bodies, with the attainment of their ambitions, with the perfection of the means and the glorification of their precious aims.

The artist undoubtedly tries to present the truths of life but in a different way or method from that of the thinker and the scientist. The artist appeals to our feelings and emotions, to our capacity for delight and wonder, and also to our latent feeling of comradeship with all the creations-men, birds and beasts, rocks, trees and flowers, and above all, land, water and the air—which Conrad believed to be the universal tie that links up the living with the non-living. In the case of thinkers and scientists, their ideas and facts are investigated, inquired into and challenged by all succeeding generations of the human race. But the artist is not challenged unless he presents some false picture of life. Conrad says in this connection that confronted by the same enigmatical spectacles, the artist descends within himself, and in that lonely region of stress and strife, if he is deserving and fortunate, he finds the terms of his appeal. His nature which, because of the war-like conditions of existence, is necessarily kept out of sight within the more resisting and hard qualities, like the vulnerable body within steel armour. His appeal is less loud, more profound, less distinct, more stirring and sooner forgotten. Yet its effect endures forever.

The changing wisdom of successive generations discards ideas, questions facts and demolishes theories. But the artist appeals to that part of our being which is not dependent on wisdom, so that in us which is a gift and not an acquisition and, therefore, more permanently enduring. He speaks to our capacity for delight and wonder, to the sense of mystery to the latent feeling of fellowship with all creation and to the subtle but invincible conviction of solidarity that knits together the loneliness of innumerable hearts, to the solidarity in dreams, in joy, in sorrow, in inspirations, in illusions, in hope, in fear; which binds men to each other, which binds all humanity, the dead to the living and the living to the unborn. Conrad's aim is to seek the truth of life, to help the readers in catching the rhythm, the music, the groans and lamentations of life, or in other words, to make the readers feel the pulse, the attention and restlessness of life; and on top of all, to present or prove the invincible bonds of friendship and solidarity which run through mankind in all ages. Let us see what Conrad himself says in this connection:

> "My task which I am trying to achieve is, by the power of the written word to make you hear, to make you feel—it is before all, to make you see. That and no more, and it is everything. If I succeed, you shall find there according to your desires: encouragement, consolation, fear, charm—all you demand, and perhaps, also that glimpse of truth for which you have forgotten to ask.

To snatch in a moment of courage, from the remorseless rush of time, a passing phase of life is only the beginning of the task. The task approached by to tenderness and faith is to hold up unquestioningly, without choice and without fear, the rescued fragment before all eyes and in the light of a sincere mood. It is to show its vibration, its colour, its form; and through its movement, its form and its colour, reveal the substance of its truth—disclose its inspiring secret; the stress and passion within the core of each convincing moment. In a single-minded attempt of that kind, if one be deserving and fortunate, one may perchance attain to such clearness of sincerity that at last the presented vision of regret or pity, of terror or mirth, shall awaken in the hearts of the beholders that feeling of unavoidable solidarity; of the solidarity in mysterious origin, in toil, in joy, in hope, in uncertain fate which binds men to each other and all mankind to the visible world."[23]

Joseph Conrad believes that man lives in society, and that there is a sense of community in him, that man is linked up with other men by a common bond of solidarity; and it is the job of the artist to awaken in man the feeling of solidarity which may be lying dormant in him or which may be temporarily concealed or suppressed by the various selfish desires of man. He further believes that it is through the fleeting moments of mental and bodily existence that man achieves the aim of his life, and the artist too achieves the aim or purpose or mission of his art. Conrad again tells us that in order to achieve such aim, the artist has to give up rule for that although he has to take the help of all the rules and all the formulas so far followed or applied by the various artists in the same field. We must examine what Joseph says regarding this warning to all of us against the pitfalls into which an artist may get entangled:

> "It is evident that he who, rightly or wrongly, holds by the convictions expressed above cannot be faithful to anyone of the temporary formulas of his craft. The enduring part of them—the truth, which each only imperfectly

veils—should abide with him as the most precious of his possession, but they all: Realism, Romanticism, Naturalism, even the unofficial sentimentalism (which, like the poor, is exceedingly difficult to get rid of); all these gods must, after a short period of fellowship, abandon him—even on the threshold of the temple—to the stammering of his conscience and to the outspoken consciousness of the difficulties of his work. In that uneasy solitude the supreme cry of Art for Art, even loses the exciting ring of its apparent immorality. It sounds far off. It has ceased to be a cry, and is heard only as a whisper, often incomprehensible, but at times, and faintly, encouraging.

Sometimes stretched at ease in the shade of roadside tree, we watch the motions of a labourer in a distant field, and after a time, begin to wander languidly as to what the fellow may be at. We watch the movements of his body, the waving of his arms, we see him bend down, stand up, hesitate, begin again. It may add to the charm of an idle hour to be told the purpose of exertions. If we know he is trying to lift a stone, to dig a ditch, to uproot a stump, we look with a more real interest at his efforts: we are disposed to condone the jar of his agitation upon the restfulness of the landscape; and even, if in a brotherly frame of mind, we may bring ourselves to forgive his failure. We understand his object, and after all, the fellow has tried, and perhaps he had not the strength, and perhaps he had not the knowledge. We forgive, go on our way—and forget. And so it is with the workman of art. Art is long and life is short and success is very far off. And thus, doubtful of strength to travel so far, we talk a little about the aim, the aim of art, which like life itself, is inspiring, difficult-obscured by mists. It is not in the clear logic of a triumphant conclusion: it is not in the unveiling of one of those heartless secrets which are called the Laws of Nature. It is not less great, but only more difficult."[24]

In this way a real artist is not an escapist. His feet are firmly transplanted in the mother earth. He is not a formalist and he seeks to harmonise the claims of form and content in his work. Let us see the concluding remarks of Conrad regarding a real artist:

"To arrest, for the space of a breath, the hands busy about the work of the earth, and compel man entranced by the sight of distant goals to glance for a moment at the surrounding vision of form and colour, of sunshine and shadows: to make them pause for a look, for a sigh, for a smile—such is the aim, difficult and evanescent and reserved only for a very few to achieve. But sometimes, by the deserving and the fortunate, even that task is accomplished. And when it is accomplished—behold!—all the truth of life is there: a moment of vision, a sigh, a smile—and the return to an eternal rest."[25]

There is no doubt in it that Joseph Conrad is a great realist and also a great romantic. He believes in facts as well as imagination, each of which should play upon the other in order to produce a good piece of art. In almost all his works, Conrad has drawn, used and reflected the experiences of his own life. He does not believe in the impersonal order of art which has been championed by the naturalists. The novels or stories of these naturalists are examples of the worst vices of the old convention of arbitrary omniscience in fiction. Conrad believes that there should be a real presentation of life with the principles of human solidarity and fidelity. So, a mere entertainer or a non serious writer, who does not care for the truths of life is no literary. But Joseph Conrad in his novels or stories used his vast experiences of life, particularly of sea life, which have entered the very web and woof of all his works of art.

References

1. Moody, Lovett, A History of English Literature, p. 382-83.
2. Gustav, Morf, 'The polish Heritage of Conrad', p. 502.
3. Najder, Zdzislaw, 'Concepts of Man and Society', p. 77.
4. Arnold, Kettle, 'An Introduction to English Novel', Vol. II; p. 67.
5. I. Howe, 'Politics and the Novel'; p. 76-113.
6. A. Zleishman, 'Conrad's politics', p. 231.
7. 'A Personal Record', Dent collected Edition, p. 97.
8. Norman, Sherry, 'Joseph Conrad: A commemoration', p. 80.
9. *Ibid.*, p. 81.
10. 'Portraits from Memory', p. 82, 84.
11. J. Conrad, 'Lord Jim', p. 147.
12. Zdzislaw, Najder, 'Concepts of Man and Society', p. 82.
13. N, Sherry, Joseph Conrad: 'A commemoration', p. 84.
14. Conrad, Joseph, 'Heart of Darkness'.
15. Conrad, Joseph, 'A personal Record', p. 134.
16. *Ibid.*, 'Preface'.
17. Najder, Zdzislaw, 'Concept of Man and Society', Macmillan P. Ltd. p. 84.
18. Albert, E., History of English Literature, Kalyani publishers, p. 70.
    Conrad, Joseph, Life and Letters, Orient Longman, p. 40.
19. Ward, A.C., Twentieth Century Literature, Orient Longman.
20. Conrad, Joseph, Nostromo, Surjeet publications, 'Preface'.
21. Conrad, Joseph, 'Victory', Orient Longman, p. 4.
22. Sherry, Norman, Joseph Conrad: A Commemoration, Macmillan; p. 138.
23. Conrad, Joseph, the Nigger of the Narcissus, Surjeet Publication, 1989, p. 7-8.
24. *Ibid.*, p. 8-9.
25. *Ibid.*, p. 9.

3

Manner of Expression

"Conrad works as an impressionist, he moves as a psychologist and he writes as a realist."[1] Hence his novels are realistic, they represent both the inner and outer realistics. He handles his novels to create atmosphere and gives a sense of depth and reality to the characters. He exploits even the supernatural to make his plots more successful and dramatic. Conrad believed that "a novel should be the biography of a man or of an affair, and biography should be a novel."[1]

Though belonging to the 20th century and a contemporary of H.G. Wells, Bennet and Galsworthy, Conrad is a unique phenomenon in the history of English novel. He was Pole by birth and did not know a word of English language with distinction. He was not a materialist but a spiritualist. He was not interested in the social problems alone, but tried to explore the psyche and soul of people. Conrad was a conscious artist deeply concerned with the nature and method of his art as his letters show. His handling of the novels is artistic and tremendously powerful. 'The Shadow Line' reveals to be a master of the traditional direct narrative method, but much of his best work is in the oblique method first used in 'Lord Jim.' Presenting his material in easy, conversational manner through the medium of a spectator, such as Marlow, he gradually builds up a picture through a series of brief sense-impressions which only reveal their full significance when they finally come together into a complete whole."[2] Such a method makes greater demand upon the reader than the simple direct narrative, but is ideal for the kind of psychological investigation in which Conrad was interested, as well as for the creation of a subtle all—pervading atmosphere which gives the story its own unity.

The man and the myth have become part of the novels of Conrad. Seaman, exiles and perhaps the two most personal of English novelists, he worked and reworked his own past, and in each case the transformation had become a matter of personal integrity, so that the novels and stories, whilst rooted in history, 'would transform it from particular to general, and appeal to universal emotions by the temperamental handling of personal experience in his novels.'[3] As Conrad observed, whilst 'Publick' mind fastens on externals, on mere facts, such for instance as ships and voyages, without paying 'attention to any deeper significance they may have.'[4] For Conrad, the 'interior journey' involved struggles of such intensity that his slightest work bears the impress, even though at times he might seem to be merely hamming his way into magazines.

Conrad's stories are distinguished for certain qualities of narrative art—notably a tendency, somewhat like Meredith's and Henry James' to postpone the crisis and defeat expectation. The result is to concentrate the force of the situation in a total effect of explosive intensity. This feature of the art of the short story has been adopted by the novelist and in Conrad's case with extraordinary success. Again, he deals with characters of a powerful and bizarre originality, tested by strange conditions and extraordinary events. Above all, he handles scene with wonderful effect that significant and influential medium which we call atmosphere. 'Victory' in its slow arranging of circumstances and human forces, its prolonged tension, and its final surprising and total catastrophe is a typical example of Conrad's art in his longer work. "The Heart of Darkness" is a magnificent example of atmosphere determining the unity and total effect of the short story. The heavy tropical air of equatorial Africa broods like a miasma over the monstrous and uncouth works of nature, twisting humanity itself into similar forms of atrocious inhumanity. Conrad is a "tireless experimenter, for whom the novel is a plastic form to be reshaped in accordance with his changing intention and design."[5] H.G. Wells placed Conrad in the same category of novelists as Henry James and when Wells spoke of "their immense artistic preoccupations."[6] he was quite right.

As pointed out by A. E. Baker, he was a romantic, yet at the same time a great realist. He maintained a balance between romanticism and classicism. He regards violence as an ordinary course of man's experience. He offsets his most exotic scenes with minutely observed and sordid details. Conrad's theory is "My task which I am trying to achieve is, by power of the written word, to make you hear, to make you feel—it is, above all, to make you see."[8] He is romantic because of his exotic settings, because he is a narrator of tales of adventure and heroism amid the wildest surroundings, and of the most outlandish type of humanity. At the same time, he is a realist because he handles the novels with most meticulous accuracy, and because autobiography is the stuff out of which his tales are made. He was a realist because his creative genius, stabilized by experiences, sought some central actuality as the starting-point for all his novels. He did not invent plots, he was almost incapable of such invention. His material was reality, subjected to the transmitting processes of a lively imagination. Seeds of fact, planted in his mind, germinated under the light of his imaginative temperament, until there grew, the complete 'romantic-realistic' novel or tale. The change with facts underwent in transmission through Conrad's mind is evident.

'The Shadow Shape' of Almayer, the 'blurred outlines' of Dain Maroola, the Malayan trader and the bluish a smoky tenuity of 'The Rescue' are equally typical of the romantic diffusing tendency of Conrad's mind."[8] This softening of outlines, this modulation of the hard glaring aspect of reality, is the essence of romantic realism. Through the original fact comes to the reader with its outlines diffused, the diffusion does not pass into distortion... "His emotional attitude to his people, his love and admiration for what was good, his scorn, pity for what was bad or weak in them, his poetic relation to beauty, his passion for the sea—these things transmuted his realism. The result is the Conrad-novel, where, more than in any other English novel, romance and realism are inseparable."[9] He was again like Hawthorne in portraying the effect than an object makes upon him who observes it. So, he became a master of impressionism which is pole apart from realism."[10] Conrad mainly handles his plots in two-subjects. He chose to make his own experience of sea-life and tropical areas as the subject-matter of his novels. The back-ground of his novels is furnished by the sea and the luxuriant forests of Malaya. Another subject which Kept Conrad engaged is the principle of fidelity and faith between man and man and the distracting power of evil in human life. These two themes make Conrad a romanticist and a moralist and both these strains run through his work.

Conrad was the first novelist who attempted with success in English to make the novel a work of art in the full and exact sense, following the example of the anglicized-American Henry James, whose manner was, however, less robust and vigorous. "In cultivating the literary art Conrad did not abate the tremendous living intensity and spiritual depth which make his novels unique."[11] Conrad believed that the style of a novel "most strenuously aspire to the plasticity of sculpture, to the colour of painting, and to the magic-suggestiveness of music which is the art of artrs."[12] He was quite conscious of his manner; he has given a theory of it. This is the direct echo of his inevitable preference; but one feels that it was encouraged as well by the doctrines of Maupassant and Flaubert. Art is self-sufficient; the artist has no object but to fully transmit the impression of reality; and the senses are the best, or rather the only way open to this expression. Therefore, the novelist must draw from all the resources of arts, whether of colour and shape or of sound; his work should have the bright hues of painting, the solidity of sculpture, the rhythm and harmony, of music. He has fulfilled this programme to the letter, not with painstaking accuracy, but with a sovereign case of a talent which when obeying rule is but following its own instinct. Handling of his novels is rightly stylistic, broadly speaking, an artificer of splendid periods, and an evoker of atmosphere, a translator of concrete phenomenon into living words. His prose is rich, glowing, atmospheric, eloquent and superb. His prose style is, in reality, the translations of thoughts, feelings, and perceptions into words with the minimum loss of intensity. His is a style of extreme flexibility, expressiveness and interest.

Conrad's style has a rich descriptive power. He can describe colour-fully and vividly an emporium in Soho in 'The Secret Agent', a luxuriant jungle-scene, sunrise and all. Similarly Panama's interrupted voyage across the Arabian Sea is the amazing description. The scenes which he calls up are varied; but their succession naturally finds a centre in the image of the sea. The registration of lights, sounds, odours and tastes is with Conrad's characters a constant automatic activity, which none of the emotions of life can interrupt. "The artist who has fixed so many sensations, and found the most fitting words to express them, has contributed, along with Kipling, to broaden the descriptive range of the English language."[13]

Conrad is the laureate of sea-life. But instead of photographically presenting sea-life and the life of jungles with extreme realism, Conrad sought to interpret the sea-life and the life of forests, and through the colour of his cosmology, gave the impressions that of life. He was again, like Hawthorne in portraying the effect that an object makes upon him who observes it. So, he became master of impressionism, which is pole apart from realism. To compare his descriptions of the sea with those of Cooper, who also was a sailorman, is to note the interesting difference. Conrad in "The Niger of the Narcissus" looks within to portray the effect of the lovely sea on his characters. Cooper, in 'The Red Sea', looks out with the ever youthful eyes of a sailor to portray the sea itself."[14]

Conrad's subject was life of the tropical forests and Malayan islands as he had viewed them, but this reality was coloured by his imagination making Conrad as a realist with a romantic outlook. His 'romantic realism' is what impresses us in his works. He was a realist because his "creative genius, stabilized by experience, sought some central actuality as the starting point of all the stories."[15] He did not invent plots. He was almost incapable of such invention. His material was reality, subjected to the transmuting process of a lively imagination. "Seeds of fact, planted in his mind, germinated under the light of his imaginative temperament, until there grew the completed 'romantic-realistic' novel or tale."[16] His actualities and facts become clothed with romantic glamour and adventurous exaltation. "It was more enduring than the excitement of romanticism of the common type because the imaginative treatment of truth is, in the long run, more satisfying than invention".[17] Hence, Miss Ruth M. Stauffer has rightly labelled Conrad as a 'romantic realist'. He was born romantic but made realist. He has the romanticist's admiration for nature, for the wilds of the sea, for loneliness, suffering and melancholy. Like a romanticist, again, he is a lover of beauty and freedom. In his works, we find the idealism of a romanticist, but he is a true portrayer of sea and situations. He observes life realistically and regards it as a union of joy and sorrow. Hence he is a romantic-realist.

Conrad was essentially the novelist of the sea and tropical jungles. He did not love the sea, though he was fascinated by it. "Impenetrable and heartless, the sea has given nothing of itself to the suitors for its precarious favours for all of its fascination that has lured so many to a violent death."[18] His own experience of the sea and, in particular, of Malayan waters, stood him in good stead as a writer, and his novels richly present the settings and environment of the tropical jungles and the pacific islands. His world is "the vast unknown nature, at once behind all things and objectified in them".[19] Storms at land as well as at sea, heroism and plotting villainy, all the ardour's and endurances of sea-faring constitute his material. But Conrad went deeper into the study of his material of sea-life and projected it in relation to human beings and their reactions to the sea-life. It is the drama in the soul that Conrad is concerned with, the mysterious seed of which of these events are the strange, the lonely, the crude or the fantastic blossoms. What intimately engages him is not the external conflict, the movement of the material universe, but the response of the mind to these invasions from without. His storms, the most wonderful things of the kind in our literature, have, therefore, an immense significance, the physical battle between man and the hostile elements being in some sort a vast and satisfying symbol of a warfare still more sublime. The whole adventure of human life is seen as a ship of souls, "voyaging strange seas of thought alone, moving from mystery to dark mystery, at once heroic and forlorn."[20]

To quote Walter Allen, "mostly while handling his work, the theme is Man against himself, the environment whether sea or exotic place, having a double function, to isolate the character from society and the larger world of men, so that he can put in extremes, and to act as the agent of his self-confrontation. Nature itself can then become a symbol of evil; or rather nature and the human being appear to exist almost as manifestations of each other." Conrad handled his novels with yet another kind of realism. His scenes are laid in Ships and outlandish foreign parts and trading posts along tropical rivers, where Europeans and native people were thrown together and had to find what accommodation they could reach with each other the pursuit of their several purposes. In the words of T.G. Williams, "the romantic suggestion is supplied by the half lights which play about the character of the novels, allowing us only fitful glimpses as we strive to penetrate the mystery which surrounds them. For Conrad, who was a Polish origin, English was an acquired language. Though he mastered it perfectly, he used it with more conscious art than an Englishman naturally would."

The modern novel is not merely an entertainment, not merely a light story meant for after-dinner reading. It is like a well-cut garden rather than a tropical jungle. Henry James was to concede that the English novel was not "necessarily the worse for the fact that it proceeded from not special theorizing. But the English novel was 'naif', and James was himself too much the artist to rejoice in the 'comfortable, good-humoured feeling' so widely held that "novel is a novel, as a pudding is a pudding, and that our only business with it could be to swallow it."[22] Conrad derived his theories from James and the 19th century French novelists, a fountain-head. As Albert points out, "James and Conrad evolved techniques which revolutionised the form of the novel. Basically they amount to an abandonment of the direct and rather loose biographical method in favour of an indirect or oblique narrative with a great concern for the aesthetic consideration of pattern and composition and a new conception of characterization built upon the study of the inner consciousness. Disproportionate attention is being given to theories of fiction; the novel is now judged by severely aesthetic consideration. Narration, description, style, must satisfy high and exacting technical methods. More, it also embodies the writer's philosophy of life, his message, his view of the human scene.

For the novelist, the problem of securing impersonality for his art has a special connection with management of the point of view. How does the narrator avoid introducing himself into the work? How, when there is information to be conveyed, can he avoid seeming to lecture his reader? How can he avoid spoiling a powerful scene by seeming to bob up before the reader like a prompt clerk? These were questions that concerned James and Ford. According to Ford, Conrad with whom he collaborated on two or three novels were to give particular attention. Conrad wished to make the reader forget the writer altogether so that the story would seem to tell itself and develop with its own life. The novelist was not to tell the reader about what happened but to render it as action. Moreover, the action was not to be rendered with photographic fidelity but as it would make its impression upon a human observer. As Ford put it, "Conrad found salvation, not in any mechanical form, but in the sheer attempt to produce in words life as it present itself to the intelligent observer."[22] Or as Conrad himself put it in his Preface to 'The Nigger of Narcissus,' 'before all, to make you see.' This device of incongruous juxtaposition became the "Time-shift" developed by Conrad and Ford. Conrad likened the effect of simultaneity gained by the time shift to the effect experienced by a person looking out of a window "through glass so bright that whilst you perceive through it a landscape or a backyard, you are aware that, on its surface it reflects the face of a person behind you."[23] Joyce, of course, exploited the device to the limit in his Ulysses". But it is by no means confined to modern fiction. Frank finds it throughout in modern poetry, in Pound's 'Cantos' and Eliot's "Waste Land", where the poet makes use of a "deliberate disconnectedness" and "superimposes one time scheme upon another."[24]

Joseph Conrad, remarkable, though not unique, even in his own time, is a complete foreigner who chose to write novels in English. People quote Conrad as an astonishing case, and forget his contemporary Maarten, a Dutchman who wrote many novels, among them 'God's Fool' is unimpeachable English; but Conrad's nature was intensely artistic. He drew most richly. He perceived finely and instinctively fashioned his impression into shapes and scenes. Thus Joseph Conrad, according to Legouis and Cazamia "is the most eminent symptom of what the new literary cosmopolitanism of the twentieth century might become—if this vien is destined to grow broader."[25]

They continue to argue about the language problem in this way:

> "No one before him had so definitely broken the tight link which binds the artistic handling of a given tongue to the exclusive possession of an intellectual nationality. The language of his childhood and youth was Polish; it remained that of his inner speech, except in moments of literary labour, when French stepped into its place. He was strongly influenced by the literature of France, and his technique is derived from that which was taught by our realists. English first studied in books, then fully adopted by this mature personality, is the instrument of expression which his art employed in the process of explicit realization.

And yet, thanks to an exceptional gift of assimilation, this instrument has the most extensive range. Conrad's vocabulary shows all the concrete wealth of the Anglo-Saxon stock; he displays in some fields at least, a rare virtuosity in the use of technical terms; his knowledge of the things and words of sea—with which he is most intimately familiar-exceeds that of Kipling. He knows, at need, how to seek effects in the ample dignity of local vocables. So glowing, luxuriant and habitual is this delight in words, that it reveals, through its very development, a constant apprenticeship of language, a manifest and all—comprehensive mastery: that abnormal something, to which, on English soil, the expert and complacent handling of linguistic resources seems to point. In fact, Conrad's prose style, at least during the early part of his career, would leave upon Britishers an impression of slightly exaggerated sonorousness and rhythm."[26]

Born in 1857 in Poland Conrad became a British subject in 1886. He is a successful illustration of foreigner, writing in English. He is the solitary instance of a foreigner writing works of genius in English and his foreignness is enough to explain all that seems strange or anomalous even in that large part of his fiction which is concerned with English characters. Under the guardianship of his maternal uncle, Thaddeus Bobrowski, under troubling pangs of the memory of his deceased father, in loneliness and desolation, Conrad became fond of reading books. He read Victor Hugo, Cerventes, Dickens, Scott and Thackeray by the time he was only ten. He read French and Polish writers too. At eleven he was enrolled at St. Anne High School in Cracow where he studied classics and German. By this time, he was familiar with French, in which he became fluent in later years. Although he learnt English quite late, he became almost prefect in this language. "It is essential to Conrad's intention that there should be no dubeity about the setting of the novel. The relationship between background and characters must be fully unambiguously established."[27]

Such a form was not open to Conrad; his particular insulating force lay in the use of the English language—a language learned only in manhood, which sometimes betrayed him into magniloquence, at other times into a painful jocularity. This accent of jaunty assurance can be heard from time to time in 'A personal Record'. It is that of a foreigner trying desperately to be at home.

M.C. B radbrook tells this realization in the following lines:

> "It can be heard in Lowry the schoolboy, and is caught dramatically in his last novel, where the undergraduate taunting his despairing friend into suicide is recalled: All right, Mr. Peter Bloody Cordwainer ... Go ahead and do it. Grandmother won't let you down, I' m sure ... she's got a lot of friends in high office. And besides, the Tibetans say you can be comfortable even in hell, just so long as you're clever. As you are, if not so damn clever as you used to be.[28]

Bradbrook continues to say that at the age of seventeen Lowry left his public school to take a voyage as a deck—hand to Yokohama via Port Said and Penang; he had told newspaper reporters, "no silk cushion youth for me. I want to see world and rub shoulders with its oddities and get some experience."[29]

This voyage gave the basis of his first novel 'Ultramarine', heavily laced with borrowings from a young Norwegian novelist who had also gone to sea to gain experience.

With this we find Barbara Kocowna pointing out that Conrad spoke Polish, French and English, learning the latter late in life and sees the problem of language as one intimately linked with the questions of loyalty, involvement and alienation which, as they form part of Conrad's psyche, are part also of his works.

Moreover, Conrad uses visual images and symbols to convey his meaning. His slogan was that "fiction must aspire to the plasticity of sculpture, to the colour of painting, and to the magic-suggestiveness of music, by the power of the written word, to make you hear, to make you feel ... before all to make you see."[30]

His own novels live upto this theory. Rightly J. Hillis Miller has suggested that Conrad wanted his readers to see beyond the merely illusive reality.

Now coming to the letters of Tadeusz Bobrowski to his nephew are an excellent and recognised source of material for Conrad's biography. However, they contain items of great interest to which so far little attention has been paid. The things referred to are Conrad's glosses on the letters in his own hand. Sometimes, they supply a commentary on dramatic conflicts arising from the exchange of ideas between two men who were closely related and yet lived so far from each other; at other times they point out the geographical situation of the sailing pedlar on the seas. They may appear as symbol or, at any rate, a forecast of decisive changes in the life of the Pole from Ukraine who entrusted his fate to favourable or unfavourable winds. The most striking thing about the glosses is the fact that they were all written in French.

That they should have been written in French is quite characteristic. It seems highly probable that at that time it was the language in which Conrad most easily expressed his thoughts. In spite of the fact that Conrad left the country five years ago he did not forget his native language. This was written to Buszczymki by Bobrowski in 1879. Actually he became accustomed to use French every day because of his French association at that time. Although Conrad wrote to his uncle in Polish, he seldom used that language at that time. He struggled hard to learn English because he wanted to pass his examinations to become an officer in the merchant navy.

The glosses prove that French was the most convenient language for Conrad to use and that he had spoken it with the greatest fluency for a long time. These are two large volumes of his letters collected from different periods which were written in French, and among all those that have been preserved, there are considerably more French than in Polish. Still it must be taken into account that the letters to his uncle written during Conrad's youth have been lost and that no trace of them remains. It is true that Bobrowski was pleased with Conrad's Polish, that he blessed him for forgetting his native language and praised his skill in holding it, though in a letter of May 26, 1882 he did correct Conrad's Polish. Three years later Bobrowski was still praising him for the correctness of his Polish, but a year later when a plan was being considered for establishing the trading company, Barr, Moering and Korzeeniowski, and it was suggested that the folders to be circulated among the gentry should be written in French and Polish. Bobrowski wrote that the text should be written by Conrad because they might be in good Polish language. This proves that Conrad must have shown, by that time, a good admixture of both French and English. Actually Polish was the native speech of the novelist, the language of those closest and dearest to him, although he had no contacts whatever with day-to-day Polish as it was heard and spoken. He was born philologist but he turned fervently to the study of English. He could master the new language for himself by his own effort just as he could get the life of a sailor for himself. It was very painful for him the experience of adapting to a new environment because he had been an over sensitive, patriotic man who remained, inspite of his young age, very much of Poland. Conrad was conservative in the noblest sense of the word. As a conservative gentleman from Eastern borderland, he retained the nineteenth century way of thinking and in particular, Polish way of thought on non-political matter.

Joseph Conrad was loyal to the generation which had brought him up. He came out in the world equipped with their outlook and their ideas firmly implanted in his mind, and these formed a kind of stereotype for him. This influence is clearly visible in his idea about U.S.S.R. He always considered himself different from any Englishman. There is no doubt in it that he had a complete command of English. But whenever he became emotional he used to speak English with great difficulty. Then he used to exclaim in Polish and French with the result that everybody failed to understand him.

This can be further illustrated in 'Amy Foster' whose autobiographical character has never been questioned. This was confirmed in his wife's memoirs. Barbara Kocowna says:

"Conrad heard Polish voice in his soul; he dreamt of Poland, and 'being emotionally a conservative-remained always a Pole even while everything in his everyday life was alien to him. His uncle's repeated admonitions to bear in mind the dignity of the nation and families to which he belonged were for Conrad-engaged at that time in struggle to be naturalised in an alien country—the proverbial drop that caused an ocean of bitterness to overflow. Conrad Korzenioski could not see himself returning to his country; the years at sea had developed his in-born love of freedom, which he was unable to renounce. He appreciated the fact that as a Pole and as a sailor he had access to anywhere in the world. However, naturalism was an absolute necessity. Bobrowski enthusiastically welcomes his 'Britisher'; for Conrad it was a move which made life simpler in one sense but still more complicated in another. He was quite free, after that, to visit his uncle without any fear for his personal safety, even it meant going as far as the Ukraine; but it represented a definite break with the past".[31]

In this way the problem of language continued but 1886 was quite important for Conrad because in this very year he passed his examination of first mate as a master mariner. In this very year he became a naturalised British subject and wrote a short story in English, "Black Mate." Now let us see what Kocowna says:

"It was clearly a trial of his strength. But had he renounced the Polish language? To think so would be a misunderstanding. When he left his country twelve years earlier with a parcel of Polish books, what could Conrad have known of the familiar sufferings of wanderers in foreign lands, of the feeling of alienation, of the nostalgia? Certainly nothing at all. He still felt very much stranger in 1886; how did he feel living in a society which was not only unable to understand him but seemed to be positively afraid of him."[32]

The story from "Amy Foster" is linked with the story in "The Secret Sharer" in a strange way. Here the protagonist presents his alter ego, a young man who is being hidden, whose presence is to be kept secret from the ship's crew. The reason for the captain allowing him to stay on board would be beyond the understanding of a common sailor on duty. This alter ego is an emanation of the artist's inner self. The same problem of alienation of a still greater solitude in a new role is given wider scope in Conrad's "Chance". Barbara Kocowna in the critical essay, 'The problem of language', said that for reasons known only to the skipper he was not satisfied by the favourable circumstances of his real life. He had got what he wanted, but along with the feeling of having achieved everything, was one of having lost everything. The literal interpretation of this atmosphere seemed impossible and for Conrad himself it had been a matter of feeling rather than of rational understanding. His own comment was that all his subconscious skill must have left him. What was it that Conrad had to hide? Obviously matters of great complexity, equal to those of the tangles of misunderstandings in 'Chance' and 'The Secret Sharer.'

"With his sensitive conscience and his uncle's admonishments to keep up the dignity of his nation and his families in mind, Conrad felt guilty in exactly the same way as that officer in 'The Secret Sharer'. The reader's sympathy is on the side of the guilty man; but he is guilty. He must hide his crime. Conrad's guilt cannot be explained here by straight analogy—and yet he calls the hidden man his ally. He had entered into an alliance with those whose paths through life cannot be simple any longer, but must remain confused until the very end. One may ask whether putting such a great distance between oneself and one's own country could be considered an act of betrayal. No reader of Conrad would do him the justice of condemning him on this ground; and yet the writer himself had done so in his conscience. At the same time he realized that it was upto him to make a decisive move; he had to give up being alien to take roots in his environment, and he succeeded in doing so after a time. But he had come near to wrecking his ship and sinking all of his crew. The loyalty of those strangers, their obedience, discipline and goodwill made him feel one of them.

Probably the torment resulting from this mood was of Conrad's long unravelled secrets; probably it was difficult for him to share his impressions even with his uncle, for obviously, he could not object to what he had achieved.' He had wanted a new life, and he simply had to accept it. His feeling of restlessness came to him at first as too great surprise for him to realise exactly what it involved; the proof of which can be found in his persistence in a state of mind which bordered on madness. Moreover, his uncle belonged to an older generation well accustomed in face of disappointments, to saying ironically to themselves and others, "Tu Nas Voulu, Georges Dandin". In this case Conrad could not manage to be ironical. He felt cruelly cheated by fate. It was only the deepest sympathy with man in a general sense which he had learnt in Congo—and his meeting a real Almayer that released his understanding of life's complexities and the simplicity of its few truths, one of which was loyalty".[33]

Conrad started spinning and weaving his visions of ships and people that he had intimately known or which attracted his attention in any way. Ultimately a Polish wrote novels and short stories in English inspite of the fact that he used to dream and think in his native background. Conrad learnt it as the only language which he could use to communicate as a sailor and the language of common people of sailors—allowed him to master this in all the wealth of its idiom. After scrutinizing the letters of Waclaw Sieroszewski, it is found that in his case the process involving the loss of his native language and the loss of contact with Poland is much more clear-cut and less complicated than in that of Conrad. Sieroszewski lived in Siberia from 1878 to 1891, after being deported for his participation in the workers' movement. Living in poverty and hardship in the cold climate of Siberia, working as a farmer, hunter and poultry farmer, he also tried his hand at literature and study. This reflection of his experience is found in his letters to his sister. All these letters were published in 1964.

Thus Conrad overcame all kinds of language problem, handled his novels and other writings in English in a much better manner than many to go deep into the minds of all common people as well as intelligentia. No one has created more convincingly the magic of the sea as Conrad did while handling his novels in a complex manner like Henry James and Ford Madox Ford—his contemporaries. His descriptions throb with the very sweep of its waves, with the very illusions of its calms. His seas are real and the whole life of sailors is portrayed with the uttermost depth of poetical reality. The august splendour of the sea is enshrined forever in the stories of Conrad. For if, in his descriptions of the hearts of men or wilds of the forests or the streets or cities, there creeps often a sense of weariness, of futility and of discouragement. In his descriptions of the sea and of its life, there shines a perennial freshness and joy. In many passages in "The Mirror of the sea" and in several passages in "Lord Jim", Conrad has thrown all his passionate love of seas and ships. His "The Nigger of the Narcissus" is a great and thrilling sea epic. The mysterious appeal of the sea has not been brought out so exquisitely by anyone as Conrad. Richard Curle says that the sea is a passion which pulses in the very heart of his books, imparting to them, amidst the cynical aspects of his philosophy, a real fervour of remembrance. It is the rejuvenating atmosphere of the sea that gives to Joseph Conrad's most typical work its everlasting appeal. He has an intimate feeling for the sea, which colours his work almost as a recognized bias colours the work of some historians. Its whole life is steeped for him in a glow of incommunicable romance and affection. In treating of it, Conrad's critical sense is sometimes in abeyance before delight of his generous enthusiasm. True melancholy of philosophy does pervade his descriptions of the ocean, but it is more often the melancholy of memory than of disillusion. In spite of complex language problem his in-born love of the sea has grown stronger from year to year because this is the ideal passion, whose only reward is the knowledge of hard labour and conquest.

Conrad has no intention of merely depicting ships and the exciting incidents of life at sea. The ambition of Conrad is made of sterner stuff; he is sailing not only the ocean known to sailors but the more profound ocean of human thought. The whole adventure of human life is seen as a ship of souls at once heroic and forlorn. He is a romantic realist and talks in common people English understandable to all.

References

1. Baines, Jacelyn, 'Joseph Conrad: A Critical biography.'
2. Ford, Madox Ford, Joseph Conrad, p. VI.
3. Albert, E., 'History of English Literature.'
4. Conrad, Joseph, Life and Letters II, p. 321.
5. *Ibid.*, p. 320.
6. Wells, H.G., Joseph Conrad, p. 30.
7. *Ibid.*, p. 31.
8. Conrad, Joseph, Life and Letters II, p. 220.
9. Baken, A.E., History of English Novel.
10. *Ibid.*
11. Long, W.J., History of English Novel.
12. Hudson, W.H., History of English Literature p. 283.
13. Conrad, Joseph, Life & Letters II, p. 210.
14. Cazamian, Louis, History of English Literature, p. 1334.
15. Long, W.J., English Literature, p. 121.
16. Ward, A.C., Twentieth century Literature, p. 91.
17. *Ibid.*, p. 94.
18. *Ibid.*, p. 105.
19. Conrad, Joseph, 'The Mirror of the Sea'.
20. Collins, Dr. A.C., English Literature of the Twentieth Century.
21. Bullet, Gerald, Modern English Fiction.
22. James, Henry, The Selected Letters, p. 171.
23. Ford, Madox Ford, The Art of Fiction, p. 11.
24. Ford, Madox Ford, "On Impressionism", In collected Edn. Poetry and Drama, I, p. 174.
25. Stallman, Critiques, p. 321.
26. William K. Wimsatt Jr. & Cleanth Brooks, Literary Criticism (A short History): Oxford, 1957, p. 683-84.
27. Legouis and Cazamian, Revised Edition, Macmillan India. Ltd., 1971, p. 1331.
28. *Ibid.*, p. 1331-32.

29. Kettle, Arnold, An Introduction to English Novel, Vol. II, B.I. Publication, 1978, p. 62.
30. October, Ferry, p. 68 (Bradbrook's essay: Narrative Form in Conrad and Lowry).
31. *Ibid.*, p. 132.
32. Preface of The Nigger of the Narcissus.
33. Kocowna Barbara, Joseph Conrad, Edited by Norman Sherry Unwin Brothers Macmillan, 1970, p. 195-96.
34. *Ibid.*, p. 196.
35. *Ibid.*, p. 197.

4

Sea-Novels : Critical Analysis

Lord Jim, Heart of Darkness, The Secret Sharer, The Nigger of the Narcissus, Nostromo, The Shadow Line

On October 14, 1874, two months before his seventeenth birthday, Joseph Conrad left for Marseilles and a sea-career armed with a few introductions and a small monthly allowance from his reluctant uncle. Shipping out from Marseilles, Conrad voyaged on French ships to the West Indies and to Central and South America; the frail factual basis of 'Nostromo' was formed here and it was on the Saint Antoine heading for South America that he had his first experience with gun.-running. Between voyages he found no difficulties in entering Marseilles café life. To his uncle's consternation, he spent his allowance liberally and soon went into debt. Most of his time was passed along the dogs with fellow sailors, although in his more serious moments, he attended performances of the operas of Rossini, Verdi and Meyerbeer. Conrad also travelled in higher circles; in the salon of M. Delestang, the banker with whom he had been given credit. Conrad met several Royalists, and these meetings led to his smuggling activities on behalf of the Carlist cause, activities which he related in "The Arrow of Gold" (1919). It was also here his biographer in G. Jean-Aubry, tells us that he met a mysterious girl, the Rita de Lastola of "The Arrow of Gold" with whom he had a brief love-affair. Reputed former mistress of Don Carlos herself, Rita was much sought after, particularly by a Southern American gentleman, the Blunt, of the same novel. Conrad conceiving himself as a romantic hero, as G. Jean-Aubry relates the story, fought a pistol duel with Blunt and was seriously wounded. A more recent biographer, Jocelyn Baines argues persuasively, however, that Conrad's serious wound was not the result of a duel but of an attempted suicide because of gambling debts. According to Baines, the duel was an invention of Conrad's to cover the suicide attempt, which was, of course, a moral sin for a catholic as well as a great embarrassment for his family. In any case, after his recovery, he saw no more of Rita and ended his Marseilles sojourn. Having spent four years in French merchant service, four years in which he drifted from one berth to another with no idea of advancement, Conrad shipped out English steamer, the Mavis, on April 24 1878, bound for Constantinople.

On the return of the Mavis to Lowestoft, Conrad first stepped on English soil, hardly understanding a word of the language, little past his twenty birthday. He decided as he points out in 'A Personal Record', that if he was to be a seaman, he would be an English seaman and none other. He said that it was a matter of deliberate choice. After two years in 1880 he passed the examination for third mate and subsequently in 1883 and 1886, for mate and master. Two years after and ten after entering the English merchant service, he had his first command on the Stago from January, 1888 to March, 1889.

It is not clear anywhere when Joseph Conrad began to write. In 1886, he began what is generally considered to be his first piece of fiction, a short story. "The Black Mate", unsuccessfully submitted for a prize competition in Tit-Bits. In the years 1887-88, he perhaps kept a diary, while at sea, just as he kept a Congo diary. But when he began his first novel "Almayer's Folly" in 1889, he was still a seaman and by no means a dedicated writer. Conrad himself wrote in "A personal Record":

> "The conception of a planned book was entirely outside my mental range when I sat down to write; the ambition of an author had never turned up amongst these gracious imaginary existences one creates fondly for oneself at times in the stillness and immobility of a day-dream."[1]

It was just after Conrad had begun 'Almayer's Folly' that he was made Second mate on a Congo steamer in late 1889, an expedition that became the source for 'Heart of Darkness', and perhaps had as much effect on maturing his outlook as the trip to the Sakhalin Islands had on Chekhov's. The Congo turned Conrad from the sea to a literary career. Broken in health by malarial fever, but impressed by the desolation and meaninglessness of what he had seen, he continued to write while recuperating.

When his heath permitted, he returned to sea on the Torrens until July 26, 1893. It was as chief of the Torrens that Conrad first met John Galsworthy and with this meeting their close friendship began. It was on the same ship that Conrad, on his last voyage, showed his manuscript of "Almayers' Folly" to a young Cantabrigian, W.H. Jacques, who encouraged him to finish the novel. When Conrad left the Torrens, he was never to go to sea again, although, it was not for lack of trying. 'Almayer's Folly' meanwhile, was finished and submitted to T. Fisher Unwin on July 4, 1894, where Edward Garnett, then a young publisher's reader, was greatly impressed with the manuscript. The novel was accepted and Conrad, encouraged by Garnett, soon turned to writing another. While evidence shows that Conrad was trying to obtain a command as late as September, 1898, he, nevertheless, continued to turn out nearly a volume a year for the next thirteen years.

Conrad's writing–life extended for twenty-nine years, from 1895 until his death in 1924.[2] During this period he wrote thirty one volumes of novels, short stories, essays and plays, besides many volumes of letters. Even with growing popularity he remained, nevertheless, isolated from the principal writers and movements. For a major novelist, his circle of friends, although intelligent and devoted, was curiously limited to those of the old guard, conservative and safe. There were, of course, some exceptions. H.G. Wells and Henry James among them—but they were never in the circle in the same sense as Edward Garnett, R.B. Cunninghame Graham, John Galsworthy, W.H. Hudson, Hugh Clifford or Edmund Gosse. Conrad seemed almost entirely unaware of Freud's works and the new advances in science, and entirely ignorant of Joyce, D.H. Lawrence, Virginia Woolf and other modern experiments in the novel; among contemporary authors of the first rank he knew only the work of Gide and Proust.[3]

At the beginning of Conrad's literary career, there was perhaps, little more than the force of will and ability to draw upon all sources and all experiences. His great power, like George Eliot's, lay in his ability to fashion strength of will into moral idea. His life's work was devoted to 'seeing' the moral idea from as many aspects as possible, until the idea became, as it were, the thing itself. Possibly Conrad, already in exile in a strange country, perceived early that only in this area could he realize his talent and any departure from it, he found, made him uneasy and unsure of himself.

The fiction of Conrad is essentially the representation of the life he had lived. Many of his stories grew entirely out of his own experience and even those that had their basis either in his imagination or in some once current tale he had heard and stored away in memory, are coloured by his experience and are given direction in his philosophy of life; "For Nietzsche, no less than for Conrad, the life of language was the first fact of the writing life, of what Conrad named, the life of the worker in prose".[4]

Marlow in 'Youth' is Conrad himself; the newly appointed captain in 'The Secret Sharer' faced with problems of a strange ship and strange crew also sprang full-sized from Conrad's own life. Likewise, the captain in 'The Shadow Line' fighting the discouraging battle against an epidemic of tropical fever is Conrad. The story found in 'Typhoon' is largely an imaginative one, although Conrad had been told the story of a steamship, full of coolies, returning from Singapore to some port in northern China. But the remarkable description of the typhoon he did create out of his intimate knowledge of the gales that menace ship in Eastern Waters. Moreover, of the captain of the Nanshan, Conrad says:

> "Mac Whirr is not the acquaintance of a few hours, or a few weeks, or a few months. He is the product of twenty years of life "My own life."[5]

Conrad, as the novelist of sea life, lived his life and then wrote and since so much of his life was lived on the sea, much of the writing of Conrad is sea stuff. Again and again the sea recurs as setting and in some of the novels, it seems to dominate. In 'The Nigger of the Narcissus' it is practically a dramatis persona. In "Typhoon", it seems like Egdon Heath in 'The Return of the Native", or better, like the great whale in 'Moby Dick' to symbolize Fate. Nor could the actual descriptions of sea be easily surpassed, the unforgettable dramatic storms of 'Typhoon' and 'The Nigger of the Narcissus'; the foaming shallow sea of 'The Rescue'; its mystery and wonder in 'The Secret Sharer'. Superficially, then, Conrad appears to belong to the long list of writers of the sea—a list including Marryat, Stevenson, and Sabtini. From the uproarious entertainment of 'Mr. Midshipman Easy', the pure adventure of 'Treasure Island' or the romance of Captain Blood, it is far cry to the subtle characterization of the captain in "The Secret Sharer" and the penetrating study of cowardice and courage in 'Lord Jim.'

For after all, Conrad is concerned primarily with men and women, whom he offers in the fullness of their being. As his handling of character is fundamentally psychological, the action in his novels proceeds from and in accordance with character. Thus it is no surprise that Arsat makes his final heroic resolution or that Mac Whirr is staunch in the face of a typhoon. Conrad never tells a story for the sake of the story alone. The element of suspense, potential in every page and culminating in a great moment of dramatic intensity, is the artistically, not merely for narrative but for character.

For Conrad, 'the interior Journey' involved struggles of such intensity that his slightest work bears the impress, even though at times, he might seem to be merely hamming his way into magazines. Taken as part of the whole work, the attentive reader may discern even in the second rate, an adumbration of the greater works. Not an artistic triumph perhaps but, 'psychological triumph of the first order… a matter of life or death, or rebirth, as it were, for its author, not to say sanity or otherwise… not Dante's personal spiritual position when he wrote 'The Inferno' was worse… the bloody agony of the writer writing it so potently extreme that it creates a kind of power in itself that, together with what humour or lyricism it may possess, takes your mind off the faults of the story itself, which, incidentally, are of every kind."[7]

This is not Joseph Conrad but Malcom Lowry on his latest work, "October Ferry to Gabriola". The completion of 'Rover' or 'Typhoon' is not the end of a tale, but the full and sympathetic comprehension of a human soul.

Albert Guerard long ago suggested that the achievement of Conrad came closer to Faulkner, Graham Greene or Malcom Lowry than to his contemporaries.[8]

On Eliot's assumptions that "comparisons and analysis are the chief tools of the critic" and that "the past should be altered by the present as much as the present is directed by the past", the reader of today who has to accommodate Henry James' 'new novel' may find in Conrad and Lowry a bridge between the two."[9]

Moreover, the development of each of these men in relation to his chosen roles interacts with his development as an artist. If Lowry's "Ultramarine"[10] may be compared with 'Youth' and 'Under the Volcano' with 'Nostromo', my main object is to correlate the works of what is often termed Conrad's decline with those of Lowry's latest phase, which have also been dismissed by many, including his biographer, as the end products of alcoholic degeneration. In particular, "October ferry to Gabriola", 'Through the Panama' and 'The Forest Path to Spring' may offer a configuration relating to 'Victory' and 'The Shadow Line.' Both depicted in the end haunted men, yet men who exercised the dark powers. And here perhaps is the place to quote a sonnet entitled Joseph Conrad written by Lowry:

> "This wrestling, as of seamen with a storm
> Which flies to leeward-while they united
> In that chaos, turn, each on his knighted,
> Bunk, to dream of chaos again, or home—
> The poet himself, struggling with the form
> of his coiled work, knows; having required
> Sea weariness with purpose, invited
> What derricks of the soul plunge in the room.
> Yet some mariners ferment in his blood
> Though truant heart will hear the iron travail.
> And song of ships that ride their easting down-
> Sustains him to subdue or be subdued.
> In sleep all night he grapples with a sail.
> But words beyond the life of ships, dream on."[11]

And Conrad wrote: "In the year 1874, I got into the train (Vienna Express) as a man gets into a dream and here is the dream going on still."[12]

His guardian and uncle had preached at him the importance of 'facts, facts, facts' and his motto was the pursuit of duty—the love of duty which circumstances define, which he opposed to grandiose ideals. Conrad took the phrase and turned it round:

> "I tell you, my friend, it is not good for you to find you, cannot make your dream come true. A man that is born falls into a dream like a man who falls into the sea. If he tries to climb out into the air, he drowns... For that, too, there is only one way... In the destructive element immerse... To follow the dream, and again to follow the dream."[13]

Even, the sea, then a word used almost synonymously with Conrad's name is incidental. He has no intention of merely depicting ships and the exciting incident of life at sea. The ambition of Conrad is made of sterner stuff; he is sailing not only on the ocean known to sailors but the more profound Ocean of human thought. The sea happens to be his raw material, just as Dorset for Hardy and New England for Hawthorne. With deliberate intention he employs the tools and medium almost available to his genius to create his interpretation of life.

Conrad's treatment of material is often called romantic realism: the realism derives from knowledge, the romanticism from feeling. In realistic description Conrad is a consummate artist. He conjures up before us with precise details the smoky, huddled forecastle of the Narcissus, the terrible rage of a typhoon, the brilliant fertility of tropical Sambir. This Conrad does with sure craft, for he knows of what he speaks. He sailed in the Narcissus; he endured storms in the China Sea; he saw Almayer in his island home. But more than mere memory of things seen was requisite of the artist. His diction tends towards both preciseness and imagery. He searches for the right word: "Give me the right word... and I will move the world." He strives to find the phrase that will express just the nuance that will harmonize with the rhythm of the whole.

In "The Secret Sharer", the beauty and suggestiveness of the opening description anticipate the sense of calm and mystery, inherent in the whole story. Even when Conrad employs abstract terms, as he often does, they are not perfunctory; they gleam with sincerity and have a significance, profound and exciting: 'O youth! The strength of it, the faith of it, the imagination of it!' So, too, his technical knowledge of sea, ships, and seamanship has the ring of truth. This technical knowledge after all, is the foundation upon which are reared such structures as 'Typhoon' and 'The Secret Sharer'; yet never is the realism obtrusive—the idiom so glitters with life and imaginative appeal.

But real as the Nan-Shan and the China Sea may be, Conrad's approach is essentially romantic. This does not mean that he is concerned merely with themes of love and adventure. As William Long puts it: "Admirers of Teodar Josef Conrad Korzeniowski, who adopted the simpler name on becoming a British citizen, are of the kind called 'few but select,' many of whom regard him as the most artistic of modern novelists."

"In speaking as he did, of 'the loneliness that surrounds every human soul, he unconsciously told what manner of man he was and what he must write. In all probability he had read Hawthorn; certainly he was like the American novelist in brooding over life as a solitude encompassed by mystery, and in portraying human events as important only in their effect on character. The scene of his story, usually the sea or a lonely island of the South Pacific, is always in harmony with his somber theme."[14]

'Victory' and 'Youth' are certainly far removed from 'Ivanhoe' and Quentin Durward. Conrad interprets life in terms of idealism. His characters are real and ideal. As Andrzej Burza puts it:

> "Unlike many modern rhetoricians, though like Cicero and Quintillion, Conrad held a holistic view of the art of writing. He did not separate the author and the work, ethics and style. He believed that, "all writing worthy of the name is temperamental".[15]

Andrzej Burza further says about Conrad' s ideology in this manner:

> "and while embracing the Flaubertian ideal that a work of fiction, like poetry should carry its justification in every line,' defined art in ethical terms, as a single minded attempt to render the highest kind of justice to the visible universe."[16]

We find the confluence of two trains of thought. One, ideological in substance, originates from a long lasting interest in Conrad's complex attitude to Russia; the other rhetorical derives from Frank Kermode's reflections on the use and usefulness of structuralist methods of analysis in the study of novels.[17]

"Initially Conrad found an area of enthusiasm that he could share with his English friends at 'Dostoyevsky Corner' as Garnett called his home: the work of Ivan Surgeyevich Turgenev, a 'good Russian', a liberal ideologically as well as artistically sympathetic to the West."[18]

We visualize white-headed, bronze faced Singleton with his spectacles and Pelham; Hays with his bald head, yellow moustache and blue eyes, Arlette dark of hair and red of mouth. We visualize his characters, we scarcely expect to encounter them. They are derived from actuality; the progenitor of Lingard and Peyrol is a Padrone of the early Mediterranean days of the Nigger, a black named Wait; of the narrator of 'Youth', Joseph Conrad himself. But over them has played romantic imagination of a creator, and the result is a galaxy of men and women of unusual personality and heroic proportion.

The technique of Conrad offers a two-fold obstacle to the unwary. In the first place, he makes use of the so-called retrogressive method, a method, of course, not unusual. In "Silas Mariner", George Eliot goes back sixteen years to the life of Mariner in Lantern Yard:

"It was a bright autumn Sunday sixteen years after Silas Mariner had found his new treasure on the hearth. The bells of the old Raveloe

Church were ringing the cheerful peal which told that the morning service was ended;... But it is impossible to mistake Silas Mariner. His large brown eyes seem to have gathered longer vision, as is the way with eyes that have been short-sighted in early life, and they have a less vague, a more answering look; but in everything else one sees signs of a frame much enfeebled by the lapse of sixteen years. The weaver's bent shoulders and white hair give him almost the look of advanced age, though he is not more than five and fifty; but there is the freshest blossom of youth close by his side—a blonde, dimpled girl of eighteen, who has vainly tried to chastise her curly auburn hair into smoothness under her brown bonnet: the hair ripples as obstinately as Brooklet under the march breeze, and the little ringlets burst away from the restraining comb behind and show themselves below the bonnet-crown... In the open yard before the Rainbow, the party of guests were already assembled, though it was still nearly an hour before the appointed feast time. But by this means they could not only enjoy the slow advent of their pleasures; they had also ample leisure to talk of Silas Mariner's strange history, and arrive by due degrees at the conclusion that he had brought a blessing on himself by acting like a father to a lone motherless child".[19]

In the same way Wren's Bean Geste opens with the strange events at Zinderneuf, reverts some ten or fifteen years to the childhood of the Gestes, and advances once more to Zinderneuf. But Conrad uses retrogressive method more frequently and more subtly. At the end of the first chapter of "Typhoon", Captain Mac Whirr stands in the Chart-room confronted by the fall of the barometer. Time stops. At the beginning of the fourth chapter, Captain Mac Whirr is standing still in the Chart-room, observing the steady fall of barometer. Time begins. The reader in the mean time learned an amazing account concerning the Nan-Shane, the mate, the engineer and the captain, not to forget his wife and his umbrella, is ready to observe and comprehend the acts of the characters on their approaching remarkable voyage. Again and again, through the mind of a character, we retreat to years and incidents and even thoughts in the past. Let us see how Conrad has presented the pictures of Typhoon:

> "The sea, flattened down in the heavier gusts, would upraise and overwhelm both ends of the Nan-Shan in snowy rushes of foam, expanding wide, beyond both rails into the night. And on this dazzling sheet, spread under the blackness

of the clouds and emitting a bluish glow, Captain Mac Whirr could catch a desolate glimpse of a few tiny specks black as ebony, the tops of the hatches, the battened companions, the heads of the covered winches, the foot of a mast. This was all he could see of his ship. Her middle structure, covered by the bridge which bore him, his mate, the closed wheel house where a man was steering, shut up with the fear of being swept overboard together with the whole thing in one great crash—her middle structure was like a half tide rock awash upon a coast. It was like an outlying rock with the water boiling up, streaming over, pouring off, beating round-like a rock in the surf to which shipwrecked people cling before they let go only it rose, it sank, it rolled continuously, without respite and rest, like a rock that should have miraculously struck adrift from a coast and gone wallowing upon the sea."

The Nan-Shan was being looted by the storm with a senseless, destructive fury: try sails torn out of the extra gaskets, double-lashed awnings blown away, bridge swept clean, weather-cloths burst, rails twisted, light-screens smashed, and two of the boats had gone already. They had gone unheard and unseen, melting, as it were, in the shock and smother of the wave. It was only later, when upon the white flash of another high sea hurling itself amid ships, Jukes had a vision of two pairs of davits leaping black and empty out of the solid blackness, with one overhauled fall flying and an iron-bound block capering in the air, that he became aware of what had happened within about three yards of his back.

He poked his head forward, groping for the ear of his commander. His lips touched it—big, fleshy, and very wet. He cried in an agitated tone, "Our boats are going now, sir."

And again he heard that voice, forced and ranging feebly, but with a penetrating effect of quietness in the enormous discord of noises, as if sent out from some remote spot of peace beyond the black wastes of the gale; again he heard a man's voice—the frail and indomitable sound that can be made to carry an infinity of thought, resolution and purpose, that shall be pronouncing confident words on the last day, when heavens fall, and justice is done-again he heard it, and it was crying to him, as if from very, very far-"All right."

He thought he had not managed to make himself understood. "Our boats—I say boat—the boats, sir! Two gone!" The same voice within a foot of him and yet so remote, yelled sensibly, Can't be helped."[20]

Conrad is not irrelevant. These apparent mental digressions fill gaps of the past and assist in comprehension of character. In short, Conrad is apt to disregard the purely chronological sequence of events and to proceed rather by the wholly natural sequence of suggestion and idea.

In the second place, many of the stories are told by a narrator or even, as in 'Lord Jim', by several narrators. In McFee's 'The Harbourmaster's, Mr. Spenlove, sitting on the passenger-deck of the 'Camotan' anchored of Puerto Balboa, spins his tale of captain Fraley and his wife. Bean Geste is told in both the third and first persons. The danger in Conrad's stories, at least, is to gain credibility, objectivity and suspense. In the author's words it is in part to make unfamiliar things seem credible. So we, hearing a story from the lips of Marlow, hearing him talk in a matter of fact digressive way, are lulled into acceptance; the effect is like that of a play within a play. Again, since his characters tell the story, Conrad, the author, seems detached. In 'Lord Jim', where the purpose is clearly objectivity, the story is told in different lights through different mediums. It is for the reader to harmonize the parts and to weigh judgment.

'Lord Jim', 'The Lagoon', 'The Secret Sharer', 'Typhoon', 'The Secret Agent', 'The Heart of Darkness', 'The Nigger of the Narcissus', 'Almayer's Folly', Nostromo' and 'Victory' are fairly representatives of Conrad which include his sea novels also. They have the glamour of ships, the mystery of the sea and the resplendence of the East. Here the nobility of men's souls is tested by the conflict of love, friendship and honour. Here, too, Conrad's technique is apparent. A great deal of ' The Lagoon' is told in first person; in 'Typhoon' objectivity is achieved by analysis of the feelings of various individuals in the same situation; in 'The Secret Sharer' there is suspense, both physical and spiritual. In all, the diction combines precision with picturesqueness.

Truly, the new reader of the stories of Joseph Conrad faces an exciting experience. A new world is here, a world of ground, engaged in adventures–strange and dramatic. From the time, the first page is turned, the characters and scenes become a part of the reader's life. Let us see the impact from 'Lord Jim':

> "He was an inch, perhaps two, under six feet, powerfully built, and he advanced straight at you with a slight stoop of the shoulders, head forward and a fixed from–under stare which made you think of a charging bull. His voice was deep, loud, and his manner displayed a kind of dogged self-assertion which had nothing aggressive in it. It seemed a necessity, and it was directed apparently as much at himself as at anybody else. He was spotlessly neat, apparelled in immaculate white from shoes to hat, and in the various Eastern

ports where he got his living as ship chandler's water-clerk he was very popular."

"A water-clerk need not pass an examination in anything under the sun, but he must have Ability in the abstract and demonstrate it practically. His work consisted in racing under sail, steam, or oars against other water-clerks for any ship about to anchor, greeting her captain cheerily, forcing upon him a card—the business card of the ship-chandler–and on his first visit on shore piloting him firmly but without ostentation to a vast, cavern-like shop which is full of things that are eaten and drunk on board-ship; where you can get everything to make her seaworthy and beautiful, from a set of chain-hooks for her cable to a book of gold-leaf for the carvings of her stern; and where her commander is received like a brother by a ship chandler he has never seen before. There is a cool parlour, easy-chairs, bottles, cigars, writing implements, a copy of harbour regulations, and a warmth of welcome that melts the salt of a three months' passage out of a sea-man's heart. The connection thus begun is kept up, as long as the ship remains in harbour, by the daily visits of water-clerk. To the captain he is faithful like a friend and attentive like a son, with the patience of job, the unselfish devotion of a woman and the jollity of a boon companion. Later on the bill is set in. It is a beautiful and humane occupation. Therefore good-water clerks are scarce. When a water-clerk who possesses Ability in the abstract has also the advantage of having been brought up to the sea, he is worth to his employer a lot of money and some humouring. Jim had always good wages and as much humouring as would have bought the fidelity of a friend. Nevertheless, with black ingratitude he would throw up the job suddenly and depart. To his employers the reasons he gave were obviously inadequate. They said, "Confounded fool!" as soon as his back was turned. This was their criticism on his exquisite sensibility."

"To the white men in the water–side business and to the captains of ships he was just Jim—nothing more. He had, of course, another name, but he was anxious that it should not be pronounced. His incognito, which had as many holes as a sieve, was not meant to hide a personality but a fact. When the fact broke through the incognito, he would leave suddenly the seaport where he happened to be at the time and go to another—generally farther east. He kept to seaports because he was a seaman in exile from the sea, and had Ability in the abstract, which is good for no other work but that of a water-clerk. He retreated in good order towards the rising sun, and the fact followed him casually but inevitably. Thus in the course of years he was known successively in Bombay, in Calcutta, in Rangoon, in Penang, in Batavia–and in each of these halting places was just Jim—the water-clerk. Afterwards, when his keen perception of the intolerable drove him away for good from seaports and white men, even into the virgin forest, the Malays of the jungle village, where he had elected to conceal his deplorable faculty, added a word to the monosyllable of his incognito. They called him Tuan Jim as one might say—Lord Jim."[21]

We find Tuan Jim, the heroic coward; Peyrol, the magnanimous rover; Wait, the towering superb negro; and all the seething Malay Archipelago, Lingard's secret river, Java Sumatra and Mindanao.

Admiration for the work means respect for the man. An author, says Conrad, reveals himself in every third sentence. Conrad would bear an examination creditably. There is essential truth in McFee's dictum that the cunning, the avaricious, and the ignoble are not admirers of Conrad. Dignity and sincerity shine through his thought and expressions. He could, as he says, no more think of writing ill when he could write well than of walking lame when he could•walk perfectly. This dignity he inherited from his uncle Tadeusz Bobrowski:

> "The letters of Tadeusz Bobrowski to his nephew are excellent and recognised source of material for Conrad's biography. However, they contain items of great interest to which, so far, little attention has been paid. The items referred to are Conrad's glosses on the letters in his own hand. Some-times they supply as commentary on dramatic conflicts arising from the exchange of ideas between two men who were closely related and yet lived, so far from each other..."

The glosses prove that French was the most convenient language for Conrad to use and that he had spoken it with the greatest fluency for a long time. There are two large volumes of his letters collected from different periods which had been written in French, and among all those that have been preserved there are considerably more in French than in Polish...

Polish was Conrad's native speech, the language of those closest and dearest to him; but how distant they were. He had no contacts whatever with day-to-day Polish as it was heard and spoken. A born philologist, he turned passionate to the study of English; and he won this new language for himself by his own effort, just as he had won a sailor's life for himself. Yet how painful the experience of adapting to a new environment must have been for this over-sensitive, patriotic man who remained, in spite of his young age, very much of a Viex Polonais. He was a conservative, but in the noblest sense to the word. As a conservative nobleman from the Eastern border-land, he retained a nineteenth century way of thinking and, in particular, Polish ways of thought on political matters.

Conrad remained loyal to the generation which had brought him up. He went out into the world equipped with their outlook and their ideas firmly implanted in his mind, and these formed a kind of stereotype for him. Though his command of English was excellent, whenever his emotions were stirred he spoke of English with great difficulty, often resorting to exclamations in Polish and French, with the result that nobody could understand him. A further illustration can be found in 'Amy Forster', whose autobiographical character has never been questioned-particularly since this was confirmed in his wife's memoirs.

Conrad heard Polish voices in his soul; he dreamt of Poland, and being emotionally a conservative—remained always a Pole even while everything in his everyday life was alien to him. His uncle's repeated admonitions to bear in mind the "dignity" of the nation and families to which he belonged were for Conrad-engaged at that time in a struggle to be naturalized in an alien country—the proverbial drop that caused an ocean to bitterness to overflow. Conrad Korzeniowski could not see himself returning to his country: the years at sea had developed his inborn love of freedom, which he was unable to renounce. He appreciated the fact that as a Pole and a sailor he had access to anywhere in the world. However, naturalism was an absolute necessity. Bobrowski enthusiastically welcomes his 'Britisher'; for Conrad it was a move which made life simpler in one sense but still more complicated in another. He was quite free after that to visit his uncle without any fear for his personal safety, even if it meant going as far as the Ukraine; but it represented a definite break with the past."[22]

There remained the problem of the language. The year 1886 was decisive for Conrad. It was the year he passed his examination and obtained his certificate of first mate as a master mariner, became a naturalized British subject and wrote a short story in English, "Black Mate". According to Barbara Kocowana:

> "It was clearly a trial of strength. But had he renounced the Polish language? To think so would be misunderstanding. When he left his country twelve years earlier with a parcel of Polish books, what could Conrad have known

> of the familiar sufferings of wanderers in foreign lands, of the feeling of alienation, of the nostalgia? Certainly nothing at all. He still felt very much a stranger in 1886; how did he feel living in a society which was not only unable to understand him but seemed to be positively afraid of him?"[23]

The episode from "Amy Foster" is connected in a peculiar manner with the story in "The Secret Sharer" in which the narrator presents his alter ego, a young man who is being hidden, whose presence is to be kept secret from the ship's crew. The reasons for the captain allowing him to stay on the board would be beyond the understanding of a common sailor on duty. This alter ego is an emanation of the artist's inner self.

The same problems of alienation and of a still greater solitude in a new role are given wider scope in Conrad's 'Chance': for reasons known only to the skipper, he is not satisfied by the favourable circumstances of his real life. He has achieved what he desired to along with the feeling of achieved everything is one of having lost everything. The literal interpretation of this atmosphere seems impossible; and for Conrad himself it was a matter of feeling rather of rational understanding. His own comment was that "all his subconscious skil1 must have left him."[24]

What was it that Conrad had to hide? Obviously matters of great complexity, equal to those of the tangles of misunderstandings in 'Chance' and 'The Secret Sharer.'

With his sensitive conscience, and his uncle's admonishments to keep up the dignity of his nation and his families in mind, Conrad felt guilty in exactly the same way as that officer in "The Secret Sharer". The reader's sympathy is on the side of the guilty man; but he is guilty. He must hide his crime. Conrad's guilt cannot be explained here by straight analogy—and yet he calls the hidden man his ally. He entered into an alliance with those whose paths through life cannot be simple any longer, but must remain confused until the very end.

Prof. Barbara Kocowna thinks in this way:

> "One may ask whether putting such a great distance between oneself and one's own country could be considered an act of betrayal. No reader of Conrad would do him the justice of condemning him on this ground; and yet the writer himself had done so in his conscience. At the same time he realised that it was upto him to make a decisive move: he had to give up being alien, to take roots in his environment, and he succeeded in doing so after a time. But he had come near to wrecking his ship and sinking all of his crew. The loyalty of those strangers, their obedience, discipline and good will make him feel one of them."[25]

Probably the torment resulting from this mood was one of Conrad's long unrevealed secrets. Probably it was difficult for him to share his impressions even with his uncle for, obviously, he could not object to what he had achieved. He wanted a new life, and he simply had to accept it. His feeling, restlessness came to him at first as too great a surprise for him to realise exactly what it involved; the proof of which can be found in his persistence in a state of mind which bordered on madness. He felt cruelly cheated by fate. It was only the deepest sympathy with man in a general sense—which he had learnt in Congo and his meeting a real Almayer that released his understanding of life's complexities and the simplicity of its few truths, one of which is loyalty.

Conrad learnt English as the only language which he could use to communicate as a sailor, and the language of common people—of sailors allowed him to master it in all the wealth of its idiom.

For a deeper understanding of this problem and after scrutinizing the correspondence of Waclaw Sieroszewski, it has been found that the process involving the loss of his native language and the loss of contact with his own country is much more clear-cut and less complicated than in that of Conrad. Moreover, it can be documented with the correspondence which has been preserved. Sieroszewski lived in Siberia in 1878-91, after being deported for his participation in the workers' movement. Living in poverty and hardship in the severe Siberian climate, working as a farmer, hunter, and poultry farmer, he was at the same time trying his hand at literature and study. A reflection of his experience can be found in his letters to his sister which have been preserved in the National Library in Warsaw and were published in 1964.

But Conrad, interpreting life, presents the weak as well as the strong. Like his Nigger, he has, from a pinnacle surveyed the virtues and foibles of the world: but unlike the Nigger, he has looked with tolerance. His irony contains no bitterness, only quiet honour and sympathy for those bewildered by fate or circumstance. With true nobility and infinite compassion, Joseph Conrad accepts all mankind. He was one of us.

But one hesitates to recommend this or that novel because Conrad is not for easy reading. Few will agree with his own judgment that 'The Nigger of the Narcissus' portraying a tremendous voyage around Cape Horn, was his masterpiece; but the preface to that novel is an excellent summary of his artistic theory of fiction. One of his best characters is found in " Under Western Eyes", a novel dealing with life in the Ukrain under Tsar's domination. 'Almayer's Folly' and 'An Outcast of Islands' in some forgotten South Seaport, 'Typhoon' which gives its title to a collection of short stories, is notable for a super description of a storm at sea and his own happy story is 'A Point of Honour', 'Lord Jim' is a brilliant sea novel.

His main theme is the moral nature of man, in particular the kind of integrity which is judged by others. His settings vary from political intrigues in Czarist Russia and espionage, blackmail and murder in London to politics and revolt in South American Republic, in addition to the exotic Eastern settings or more specifically sea stories.

Let me present the critical analysis of important novels of Conrad to find out his mind and art through which the first emergence of Conradian Voice can be heard. His manner of expression points out that Conrad spoke Polish, French and English, learning the latter late in life and sees the problem of language as one intimately linked with the questions of loyalty, involvement and alienation which, as they form part of Conrad's psyche, are part also of his works.

The scenes which Conrad calls up are varied, but their succession naturally finds a centre in the image of the sea. It is from the deck of a ship that we witness the unrolling of the sights of the world, the smiles and furies of the ocean, ship board dramas, distant scenes, the landscapes and manners of Oceania of Asia, and of those English seaports whither the liners find their way back, make up an intensely vivid show which forces itself upon our view like striking, almost haunting décor. 'Lord Jim', 'The Heart of Darkness', 'Typhoon' etc. are important sea novels. Let me analyse 'Lord Jim' first.

Lord Jim

"Lord Jim" was first published in monthly instalments in the Blackwood's Magazine from October 1899 to November 1900 and was finally published in the book-form in 1900. It was originally called Tuan Jim. Tuan in Malay means "Lord" On its appearance, it was warmly appreciated by Edward Garnett, Galsworthy and Henry James. But at the same time it was also criticised. Even F.R. Levis has criticised it in 'The Common Pursuit'.[26] Nevertheless, it is one of Conrad's best works.

The chief sources of the novel are Conrad's personal experience of sea-life and his knowledge about the history and working of sea-men. The story of the Jeddah ship also inspired him to write this novel. Conrad wanted to write a novel on his own life, and 'Lord Jim' is the account of his own life given very objectively. Jim's adventure in Patusan is based in part on Conrad's knowledge of James Brooke, an English adventurer, who had adopted a fabulous career and was the subject of a number of books which Conrad probably knew well. On the technique of the novel there is an obvious imprint of Flaubert and Henry James.

Richard Curle has given the summary of the novel in the following manner:[27]

"Lord Jim was the son of an English country-parson, who was given necessary educational training to suit his career as a sea-man. Jim belonged to a middle-class family with a strong belief in character. His outlook on life was that of the most respectable man, anxious to make his mark in the world through honourable courses of conduct. Jim had a fanciful temperament and was quite often given to day dreaming. He wanted to establish himself in life as an exceptional and heroic type of man. Having passed High School Examination, Jim got training in the science of navigation. He went to a special training ship where he got the practical training in handling the ship as well as the theoretical knowledge of Mathematics, Trigonometry, and chart reading and so on. During the time of his training, a small incident occurred which touched Jim to the very core. One day, two small vessels collided, resulting in injuries to an elderly sea-man. A number of boys immediately rushed out in a boat to help them. Jim came a little too late and so could not get into the boats. As he stood at the rails, disappointed, an elderly sea-man came behind him and cheered up saying." Let us see how brilliantly Conrad describes the incident:

> "It was the dusk of a winter's day. The gale had freshened since noon, stopping the traffic on the river and now blew with the strength of a hurricane in fitful bursts that boomed like salvoes of great guns firing over the ocean. The rain slanted in sheets that flicked and subsided, and between while Jim had threatening glimpses of the tumbling tide, the small craft jumbled and tossing along the shore, the motionless buildings in the driving mist, the broad ferry-boats pitching ponderously at anchor, the vast landing-stages heaving up and down and smothered in sprays. The next gust seemed to blow all this away. The air was full of flying water. He stood still. It seemed to him he was whirled around."

"He was jostled. "Man the cutter!" Boys rushed past him. A coaster running in for shelter had crashed through a schooner at anchor, and one of the ship's instructors had seen the accident. A mob of boys clambered on the rails, clustered round the davits. 'Collision. Just ahead of us. Mr. Symons saw it.' A push made him stagger against the mizzen-mast, and he caught hold of a rope. The old training ship chained to her moorings quivered all over, bowing gently head to wind, and with her scanty rigging humming in a deep bass the breathless song of her youth at sea. 'Lower away!' He saw the boat, manned, drop swiftly below the rail, and rushed after her. He heard a splash. 'Let go; clear the falls!' He leaned over. The river alongside seethed in frothy streaks. The cutter could be seen in the falling darkness under the spell of tide and wind, that for a moment held her bound, and tossing abreast of the ship. A yelling voice in her reached him faintly: 'Keep stroke, you young whelps, if you want to save anybody! Keep stroke!' And suddenly she lifted high her bow, and, leaping with raised oars over a wave, broke the spell cast upon her by the wind and the tide."

"Jim felt his shoulder gripped firmly. 'Too late, youngster.' The captain of the ship laid a restraining hand on that boy, who seemed on the point of leaping overboard, and Jim looked up with the pain of conscious defeat in his eyes. The captain smiled sympathetically. 'Better luck next time. This will teach you to be smart."[28]

Jim's disappointment was owing to the fact that he had missed chance of taking part in an exciting adventure. Actually, it was not such a great occasion as he thought; Jim himself understood that it was a very simple affair. In his own mind, he thought that when he had his chance, he would do much greater things than the other boys.

Jim completed his training in due course of time. He became the chief mate on the pilgrim ship, Patna:

> "The Patna was a local steamer as old as the hills, lean like a greyhound, and eaten up with rust worse than a condemned water tank. She was owned by a Chinaman, chartered by an Arab, and commanded by a sort of renegade New South Wales German, very anxious to curse publicly his native country, but who, apparently on the strength of Bismarck's victorious policy, brutalised all those he was not afraid of, and wore a 'blood and iron' air, combined with a purple nose and a red moustache. After she had been painted outside and whitewashed inside, eight hundred pilgrims (more or less) were driven on board of her as she lay with steam up alongside a wooden jetty."[29]

On a calm night, in the Red Sea, while Jim on the bridge, lulled into a sense of delicious and perfect security, was waiting the end of his watch, the Patna collided with a submerged wreck. To a boat, in her condition, such a thing would have been fatal ninety-nine times out of a hundred. Not one of the eight sleeping pilgrims realised what had happened, but immediately a subdued, hideous panic broke out on the upper deck amongst the few white officers and engineers. Jim, disdainful of their terror, watched in scornful silence while they lowered a boat with feverish haste. At any instant, the bulkhead might give way. Jim himself an examination and found the plates bulging inwards. And there were no boats for the pilgrims. He watched with utter disgust the terror of the white officers, but suddenly, when the boat was already in the water, he jumped. He had not meant to do so, he was sure of himself, but at the crisis, he jumped. And it was this lapse for which all the rest of his life he had to atone, for public disgrace followed quickly upon his action. By some unaccountable fortune, the Patna succeeded in keeping afloat and it was towed into Suez by a French warship. A ship deserted by her officers was thus saved. So the, more or less, plausible story invented by the Captain, who knew that dead men tell no lies, was proved false and they were disgraced for ever.

It was at the court of inquiry that Marlow, the narrator of the tale, made acquaintance with Jim. He was attracted to him against his will, and in all Jim's subsequent wanderings of an uneasy spirit:

> "Jim's eyes, wandering in the intervals of his answers, rested upon a white man who sat apart from the others, with his face worn and clouded, but with quiet eyes that glanced straight, interested and clear. Jim answered another questions and was tempted to cry out. "What's the good of this! What's the good!" He tapped with his foot slightly, bit his lip, and looked away over the heads. He met the eyes of the white man. The glance directed at him was not the fascinated stare of the others.* Jim between two questions forgot himself so far as to find leisure for a thought. This fellow—ran the thought—looks at me as though he could see somebody or something past my shoulder. He had come across that man before in the street perhaps. He was positive, he had never spoken to him. For days, for many days, he had spoken to no one but had held silent, incoherent, and endless converse with himself, like a prisoner alone in his cell or like a wayfarer lost in a wilderness. At present he was answering questions that did not matter though they had a purpose, but he doubted whether he would ever again speak out as long as he lived. The sound of his own truthful statements confirmed his deliberate opinion that speech was of no use to him any longer. That man there seemed to be aware

* It was an act of intelligent volition.

of his hopeless difficulty. Jim looked at him, then turned away resolutely, as after a final parting.

And later on, many times, in distant part of the world, Marlow showed himself willing to remember Jim, to remember him at length, in detail and audibly."[30]

Everywhere he was dodged by some evidence, some reminiscence of that one act, and he flew from spot to spot, throwing up good and permanent jobs at the breadth of suspicion. For he was the slave of an idea—the rehabilitation. And at last, in far off Patusan, as adviser and virtual ruler of a savage and trusting people, he gained all the peace of mind that he was ever likely to know. In the sun of this colossal triumph, the shadow of his failure is hardly discernible. According to Stein's advice, Jim was sent to Patusan which was somewhere in the Archipelago, where Jim could feed his romantic spirit. But what is Petusan? Conrad has described it in this way:

> "I don't suppose any of you had ever heard of Patusan? Marlow resumed, after a silence occupied in the careful lighting of a cigar. "It does not matter; there's many a heavenly body in the lot, crowding upon us of a night that mankind had never heard of, it being out-side the sphere of its activities and of no earthy importance to anybody but to the astronomers who are paid to talk learnedly about its composition, weight, path—the irregularities of its conduct, the aberrations of its light—a sort of scientific scandal mongering. Thus with Petusan, it was referred to knowingly in the inner government circles in Batavia especially as to its irregularities and aberrations, and it was by name to some few, very few, in the mercantile world. Nobody, however, had been there, and I suspect no one desired to go there in person, just as an astronomer, I should fancy, would strongly object to being transported into a distant heavenly body, where, parted from his earthly emoluments, he would be bewildered by the view of an unfamiliar heavens. However, neither heavenly bodies nor astronomers have anything to do with Patusan. It was Jim who went there. I only meant you to understand that had Stein arranged to send him into a star of the fifth magnitude, the change could not have been greater. He left his earthly failings behind him and that sort of reputation he had, and there was a totally new set of conditions for his imaginative faculty to work upon. Entirely new, entirely remarkable. And he got hold of them in a remarkably new manner."[31]

Stein had sent Jim to Patusan to relieve Cornelius who had been working as a manager of Stein and Co. It was out of consideration for the wife and daughter of Cornelius that stein had appointed him (Cornelius) as his manager. Patusan is a distant district of a native-ruled state and the settlement bears the same name. At some point, on the river about forty miles away from the sea, the tops of two hills are visible. These hills are separated by a chasm:

> "Patusan is a remote district of native-ruled state, and the chief settlement bears the same name. At a point on the river about forty miles from the sea, where the first house comes into view, there can be seen rising above the level of the forests, the summits of two steep hills very close together and separated by what looks like a deep fissure, the cleavage of some mighty stroke. As a matter of fact, the valley between is nothing but a narrow ravine; the appearance from the settlement is of one irregularly conical hill split in two, and with the two halves leaning slightly apart. On the third day after the full moon as seen from the open space in front of Jim's house (he had a very fine house in the native style) rose exactly behind these hills, its diffused light at first throwing the two masses into intensely black relief, and then the nearly perfect disc, glowing ruddily, appeared, gliding upwards between the sides of the chasm, till it floated away above the summits, as if escaping from a yawning grave in gentle triumph. 'Wonderful effect', said Jim by my side. 'Worth seeing, is it not?"[32]

Thus we find that Jim had a house upon the space in front of one of the hills. Stein and Marlow had sent him to Patusan to get him out of the way or rather out of his own way. Marlow was going home and that is why he wanted to dispose of Jim. Marlow visits him in this distant corner of the East and finds him crowned with the prestige of an immense success. And yet the final mishap of his life is lying ready at certain adventures, a group of pirates, headed by one Brown, penetrated his settlements with blood thirsty intention. They were surrounded, cut off from supplies and could have been killed by a man, but on Jim's advice they were allowed to depart in peace to their ship at the mouth of the river. They went and Patusan rejoiced. But in their decent, as a last revenge, they murder a body of resting warriors, commanded by the son of their chief, Doramin. The story was narrated by Marlow. He related in a letter to his friend, the remarkable exploits of a man called Brown who stole successfully a Spanish schooner out of a small bay near Zamboanga. Marlow had met Brown just a few hours before his death. Marlow wrote also about Cornelius. Brown said to Marlow that Jim was a fool, a hollow sham, who had not the courage to kill him (Brown), that Jim had committed a fraud by letting off Brown for which, of course, Jim had to pay the death penalty:

> "It all begins with a remarkable exploit of a man called Brown, who stole with complete success a Spanish schooner out of a small bay near Zamboanga. Till I discovered the fellow my information was incomplete, but most

unexpectedly I did come upon him a few hours before he gave up his arrogant ghost."[33]

Marlow's story began with the story of Brown, who was supposed to be the son of a baronet. He had deserted from a home ship and became the terror of various islands in Polynesia. He kidnapped the natives and robbed the white traders. Brown was a latter-day buccaneer. He was like other notorious buccaneer such as Bully Hayes or the sweet-tongued Peace or the fashionable scoundrel Dirty Dick, but he was different from them by his arrogant temper, by his scorn for mankind in general and particularly for his victims. He used to rob a man only to demonstrate his poor opinion about the victim. When he was at the height of glory, he used to own an armed burge manned by a crew of Kanakas and run away whalers, and used to boast that he was financed by a most respectable firm of Copra merchants. He ran away with the young wife of a missionary who died on board his ship and over whom he expressed his vehement grief. He lost his ship on rocks of Malatia and disappeared for some time till he was seen at Nuka-Hiva where he purchased an old French schooner from the government. But South Seas became too hot for him. He shifted his activities to further west in Manila Bay. Thereafter he hung around the Philippines in his rotten schooner, fighting with adverse fortune till he sailed into Jim's realm-Patusan.

At that time Jim had been away in the interior for more than a week. It was Dain Waris who had directed the first repulse. Several messengers were sent out to discover the where-about of Jim. In the meanwhile, Kassim, the representative of Rajan, had managed to open communications with the besieged Brown. Kassim took Cornelius as his interpreter. Cornelius made a preliminary approach to Brown. Half an hour's talk with Cornelius opened Brown's eyes as to the home-affairs of Patusan. He became cautious at once.

Kassim disliked Doramin and his Bugis but he hated the new order of things still more. He believed that Brown, the pirate, and his men together with Rajah's followers could attack and defeat the Bugis before Jim's return. He calculated that the town folk also would later on go against Jim. In the long run, Brown and his men could be tackled because they would have no friends after the defeat of Jim and the Bugis. Kassim believed further that Brown and his men were outcasts-men without country. Brown had been urged by necessity to come to Patusan, and so he could be pleased if he could steal sufficient food and also tons of rubber or gum, together with a handful of dollars. He further thought that with the help of Jim, he could steal the whole country and then quit it. Brown enquired of Jim. What sort of a man he was, whether he was an Englishman or not. Cornelius repeatedly suggested that Brown should kill Jim at the earliest opportunity. Meanwhile Dain Warris' s fleet of canoes, stolen one by one under shore farthest from the creek and went down to close the river against Brown's retreat. Brown was not aware of this approaching danger. On Kassim's repeated request, Brown sent a man with a chit to the Chinaman of the schooner as the result of which the emissary of Kassim was entrapped in the schooner.

Brown's object was to gain time by fooling Kassim's diplomacy. He believed that Jim was not a fool and he, therefore, decided to cooperate with him and thereby become the sole monarch of Patusan, and then if necessary, he would get rid of Jim with a shot. But Brown inspite of his optimism, felt that he was really in a very tight corner and he could not think of getting out of it. One of the followers of Brown was shot dead while trying to get tobacco from the boat.

There was a good deal of noise and shouts of rejoicing on the unscalable side of the mountain. Brown came to know from Cornelius that it was all due to the arrival of Jim among his friends. When Brown wanted to know how he could contact Jim, Cornelius said Jim would be coming to Brown soon of his own accord, because Jim was not afraid of anything, just as a stupid child is not afraid of anything. Cornelius repeatedly advised Brown that he should kill Jim at the earliest opportunity:

"At last the tide flowed, silencing the plaint and the cries of pain, and the dawn was near when Brown, sitting with his chin in the palm of his hand before Patusan, as one might stare at the unscalable side of a mountain, heard the brief ringing bark of a brass six-pounder far away in town somewhere. What's this? He asked of Cornelius, who hung about him. Cornelius listened. A muffled roaring shout rolled down river over the town; a big drum began to throb, and others responded, pulsating and droning. Tiny scattered lights began to twinkle in the dark half of the town, while the part lighted by the loom of fires hummed with a deep and prolonged murmur. 'He has come', said Cornelius, 'What'? Already? Are you sure? Brown asked 'Yes! Yes! Sure. Listen to the noise. 'What are they making that row about? Pursued Brown. 'For Joy', snorted Cornelius; 'he is a very great man, but all the same, he knows no more than a child, and so they make a great noise to please him, because they know no better.' 'Look here', said Brown, 'how is one to get at him? 'He shall come to talk to you.' Cornelius declared. 'What do you mean? 'Come down here strolling as it were?' Cornelius nodded vigorously in the dark. 'Yes. He will come straight here and talk to you. He is just like a fool. You shall see; you shall see', repeated Cornelius. 'He is not afraid—not afraid of anything. He will come and order you to leave his people alone. He is like a little child. He will come to you straight. 'Alas! he knew Jim well—that 'mean little skunk', as Brown called him to me. 'Yes, certainly', he pursued with ardour, 'and then, Captain, you tell that tall man with a gun to shoot him. Just you kill him, and you shall frighten everybody so much that you can do anything you like with them afterwards—get what you like-go away when you like. Ha! Ha! Ha! Fine...' He almost danced with impatience and eagerness; and Brown, looking over his shoulder at him, could see sitting amongst the cold ashes and the litter of the camp, haggard, cowed, and in rags".[34]

Brown and Jim met just at the same spot where Jim had taken the second desperate leap of his life—the leap landed him into the life of Patusan, into the trust, the love, the confidence of the people. Brown and Jim faced each other across the creek and tried to understand each other before they spoke. Brown hated him at first sight because he had expected Jim to be at least something like him (i.e. a buccanceer) which unfortunately Jim did not appear to be. Jim asked Brown who he was and why he had corne to Patusan for food! What Brown in return asked Jim, why he had come there, Jim was a little startled. Brown said to Jim:

> "There was nothing to be shocked at in this. He had come down of his own free will. 'Let us agree', said I, 'that we are both dead men, and let us talk on that basis, as equals. We are all equal before death', I said. I admitted, I was there like a rat in a trap but we had been driven to it, and even a trapped cat can give a bite. He caught me up in a moment. 'Not if you don't go near the trap till the rat is dead. I told him that sort of game was good enough for these native friends of his, but I would have thought him too white to serve even a rat so. Yes I had wanted to talk with him. Not to beg for my life, though. My fellows were-well-what they were—men like himself, anyhow. All we wanted from him was to come on in the devil's name and have it out. 'God do it, said I, while he stood there as still as wooden post. 'You don't want to come out here every day with your glasses to count how many of us are left on our feet, come. Either bring your infernal crowd along or let us go out and starve in the open sea, by God! You have been white once, for all your tall talk of this being your own people and you being one with them. Are you? And what the devil do you get for it; what is it you've found here that so, what precious Hey! You don't want us to come down here perhaps—do you?

"That's what I told him—I knew what to say', he began again, feebly at first, but working himself up with incredible speed into a fiery utterance of his scorn. 'We are not going into the forest to wander like a string of living skeletons dropping one after another for ants to go to work upon us before we are fairly dead, oh no! "You don't deserve a better fate!" he said. "And what do you deserve", I shouted at him. "You that I find skulking here with your mouth full of responsibility, of innocent lives, of your infernal duty. What do you know more of me than I know of you?"—I came here for food. D'ye hear? Food to fill our bellies. And what did you come for? What did you ask for when you came here? We don't ask you for anything but to give us fight or a clear road to go back whence we came..." "I would fight with you now", says he, pulling at his little moustache. "And I would let you shoot me, and welcome," I said, "This is as good a jumping—off place for me as another. I am sick of my infernal luck...I am here because I was afraid once in my life. Want to know what of? Of a prison. That scares me, and you may know it—if it's any good to you. I won't ask you what scared you into this infernal hole, where you seem to have found pretty pickings. That's your luck and this is mine—the privilege to beg for the favour of being shot quickly, or else kicked out to go free and starve in my own way..."[35]

Marlow remarks in this connection:

"It is impossible to say that how much Brown lied to Jim then, how much he lied to me now—and to himself always. Vanity plays lurid tricks with our memory, and the truth of every passion wants some pretense to make it live. Standing at the gate of the other world in the guise of a beggar, he had slapped this world's face, he had spat on it, and he had thrown upon it an immensity of scorn and revolt at the bottom of his misdeeds. He had overcome them all—men, women, savages, traders, ruffians, missionaries and Jim—that beefy-faced beggar."[36]

Brown admitted to Marlow that Jim was not of the sort that could be got over by trucking and accordingly, he took care to show himself as a man confronting without dismay ill-luck, censure and disaster. Brown told Marlow that perceiving the size of the place (Patusan), he had resolved instantly in his mind that as soon as he had gained a footing he would set fire right and left, and begin by shooting down everything, living in sight, in order to cow and terrify the population. The disproportion of forces was so great that this was the only way giving him the slightest chance of attaining his ends—he argued in a fit of coughing. But he did not tell Jim this.

Brown asked Jim whether he had nothing fishy in his life to remember that he was so dementedly hard upon a man, trying to get out a deadly hole by the first means that came to hand—and so on and so on.

Jim asked, "Will you promise to leave the coast? Brown lifted and let fall his hand, giving everything up as it were—accepting the inevitable. "And surrender your arms?" Jim went on. Brown sat up and glared across. "Surrender your arms." Not till you come to take them out of our stiff hands. You think I am gone crazy with funk? Oh, no! that and the rags I stand in is all I have got in the world, besides a few more breech loaders on board; and I expect to sell the lot in Madagascar, I ever get so far-begging my way from ship to ship.

"Very well", said Jim, lifting his head suddenly after a long silence. 'you shall have a clear road or else a clear fight.' He turned on his heel and walked away."[37]

Jim said to common people who were very much agitated by the arrival of the white men and by their sporadic attacks on the natives of Patusan. 'Everybody will be safe.' Jim's mind was made up that Brown should have his way clear back to sea. Jim's fate was forcing his hand. He had for the first time to affirm his will in the face of outspoken opposition. Last of all, he turned to Doramin and said:

"Then, call in Dain Waris, your son, my friend, for in this business I shall not lead."[38]

Doramin had earlier sent a detachment of his men under the command of his son, Dain Waris, in some boats, down stream with a view to cut off the retreat of Brown as well as to prevent any further detachment of men from the ships coming in. Cornelius and Kassim had informed Brown of this. Brown felt that he was in the midst of great danger. Cornelius, however, offered to take them by line of back waters, so that they would not be exposed to the fire of Dain Waris and his men.

After his interview with Brown, Jim came back to Doramin and informed him that he had arranged for the safe withdrawal of Brown and his men and that he could depend upon Brown going away without any further trouble to them. Although many people were dissatisfied and wanted to fight Brown and his men. Doramin sent a special messenger, his own servant, Tamb Itam, with his ring in token of his authority, to Dain Waris with instructions not to attack the party of Brown, but to allow them to go away quietly. By the time, Brown, in the company of Cornelius, crossed the point where Dain Waris had the camp. It was early morning and Brown then got an original idea into his head. He felt that he could take his revenge upon the men without himself being exposed to danger. So he ordered all his men to fire at the camp of Dain waris at once and quickly. One of the bullets hit Dain Waris and he fell down dead. Tomb Itam saw this shocking sight.

After taking his revenge, Brown pushed Cornelius to the shore and sailed away. A little later, Tamb Itam came to the bank of the river and saw Cornelius in a state of terror. Tomb Itam at once guessed that Cornelius must have been at the bottom of the mischief and immediately stabbed him to death.

Tamb Itam rushed back and informed Jewel, and later on Jim of all that happened. Both Jewel and Tomb Itam urged Jim not to remain there any more, for they realised that Doramin, the bereaved father and infuriated people would blame him for this and would kill him.

Jim brushed aside their entreaties and came straight to the palace of Doramin. There he found people gathered together, mourning the death of their beloved Dain Waris. Jim walked up with grave dignity, where Doramin was seated on his throne with his wife by his side, plunged in grief. After coming close to the chief, Jim bent his head towards him and said he had come back to him to answer for the death of his son. Doramin looked at Jim, and taking his pistol, fired at him. The shot, piercing Jim's heart, killed him on the spot:

> "Doramin, alone, immense and desolate, sat in his armchair with the pair of flintlock pistols on his knees, faced by an armed throng. When Jim appeared at somebody's exclamation, all the heads turned round together, and then the mass opened right and left and he walked up a lane of averted glances. Whispers followed him, murmurs: 'He has worked all the evil.' 'He hath a charm'... He heard them perhaps!"

'He came! He came! "was running from lip to lip, making a murmur to which he moved. 'He hath taken it upon his own head', a voice said aloud. He heard this and turned to the crowd. 'Yes, upon my head.' A few people recoiled.

Jim waited a while before Doramin and then said gently, I am come in sorrow'. He waited again. 'I am come ready and unarmed', he repeated:

> "The unwieldy old man, lowering his big forehead like an ox under a yoke made an effort to rise, clutching at the flint-lock pistols on his knees. From his throat came gurgling, choking, inhuman sounds, and his two attendants help him from behind. People remarked that the ring which he had dropped on his lap fell and rolled against the foot of the white man, and that poor Jim glanced down at the talisman that had opened for him the door of fame, love, and success within the walls of forests fringed with white foam, within the coast that under the western sun looks like the very stronghold of the night.

> Doramin, struggling to keep his feet, made with his two supporters a swaying, tottering group: his little eyes stared with an expression of mad pain, of rage, with a ferocious glitter, which the bystanders noticed; and then, while Jim stood stiffened and with bared head in the light of the torches, looking him straight in the face, he clung heavily with his left arm round the neck of a bowed youth, and lifting deliberately his right, shot his son's friend through the chest.

"The crowd, which had fallen apart behind Jim as soon as Doramin had raised his hand, rushed tumultuously forward after shot. They say that the white man sent right and left at all those faces a proud and unflinching glance. Then with his hand over his lip he fell forward dead."

"And that's the end. He passes away under a cloud, inscrutable at heart, forgotten, unforgiving and excessively romantic. Not in the wildest days of his boyish vision could have seen the alluring shape of such an extraordinary success! For it may very well be that in the shortest moment of his last proud and unflinching glance, he had beheld the face of opportunity which, like an Eastern bride, had come veiled to his side."[39]

Thus Jim paid the supreme penalty with his life, and thereby proved what a man of heroic constancy and unblemished honour he was. Jim accepted responsibility for the death of Dain Waris, since it was on his advice that Doramin allowed Brown and his men to go away unmolested.

All these stirring events, pertaining to the last phase of Jim's career, were later on narrated by Jewel and Tomb Itam to Stein from whom Marlow obtain the details. Jewel and Tomb became heart broken after his death, and escaping from Patusan, arrived at the residence of Stein where they were looked after by him with his usual kindness and generosity. Thus, the career of Jim ends in a high tragedy which, though painful, is also inspiring in its own way.

The novelist seeks to present before his readers a truth about life—as it emerges out of life itself. In the novel there has always been in Jim a clash between imagination and action, between idealism and reality.

Honour and betrayal have been a constant theme with Conrad. So has been guilt and punishment. All these figure find respectable place in 'Lord Jim'. Jim betrays himself, the craft to which he belongs, as well as the pilgrims on the board. For this act of betrayal, he suffers terribly and finally at once for it by his death. The novel also exposes the dangers of excessive imagination, and suggests that human salvation lies in fidelity and duty. One of the common themes of Conrad is the incessant conflict of man with nature or with himself. In "Lord Jim," Jim is constantly at war with himself and the novel is a powerful depiction of his spiritual agony, and this makes the novel one of the greatest studies of conduct in our literature.

Heart of Darkness

'Lord Jim', 'The Secret Sharer', 'Heart of Darkness,' 'Typhoon', 'Nostromo', 'The Secret Agent' are fairly representatives of Conrad. They have the glamour of ships, the mystery of the sea and the resplendence of the East. Here the nobility of men's souls is tested by the conflict of love, friendship and honour.

Introduction: "Heart of Darkness" has a 'framed' narrative structure, meaning that one 'I' opens the story and sets the stage for the second 'I' who narrates the tale. The first 'I' speaks in first person objective; the second "I" (Conrad-Marlow) speaks in first person subjective.

The story comes out of its frame and returns to the Nellie's deck several times. Conrad's object in providing these 'returns' is to show Marlow's audience and its lack of perception. Each return entails a change of view point.

As in "Lord Jim" and other of Conrad's early works, Conrad puts two or more characters' conversations into a single paragraph. Modern writers usually separate each person's speech into separate paragraph. Many paragraphs of Conrad's are much too long. Conrad uses more punctuation than writers would use today, specially exclamation points, dashes and dots. Marlow's story is all in quotations necessitating inner quotes for all the dialogue in the story.

Although of Polish birth, Conrad learnt English thoroughly. He uses a vocabulary which any modern writer might envy. He chooses strong dramatic words. His metaphors and similes conjure up startling images. His peculiar habit of pairing adjectives occurs often in "Heart of Darkness", as it does in "Lord Jim". Typical examples are 'exuberant and entangled', "hospitable and festive", "empty and desolate." In this connection a letter to John Galsworthy, dated 17 April, 1899, Joseph Conrad observed:

"Every word is an object to be considered anxiously with heart searching's and in a spirit of severe resolutions..."[40]

Some critics object to Conrad's use of so many words which attempt to say what cannot be put into words, such as impenetrable, incredible, inextricable, inscrutable, incomprehensible, unfathomable, and most frequent of all, inconceivable. These critics feel that Conrad obscures his story with these words.

Conrad's work, however, charms his readers with its oblique approach. Examples in 'Heart of Darkness' are numerous. One excellent example is the round about method he uses to show that the manager's excuses for neglecting Kurtz are phoney. Kurtz is able to negotiate three hundred miles of the Upper Congo in a dugout canoe with native rovers. His half-caste Clerk is able to bring a fleet of ivory-laden canoe down the remaining seven hundred miles to the Central Station. The manager could have sent up a fleet of dugouts had he truly wished to relieve Kurtz.

Another example of the oblique approach is Conrad's having Marlow repeatedly use a single gesture. Marlow 'turns away'. Thus Conrad emphasizes one of his main themes: man's inhumanity to man is his greatest sin. We can find that in every instance where Marlow turns away, he is witness to senseless cruelty. Conrad uses this oblique approach to show through the attitude of Marlow's four listeners, another of his themes: materialistic minds cannot grasp, or be interested in adventures of the spirit.

"Heart of Darkness" is really two stories—(a) story of Charlie Marlow's trip from the civilization of Europe to the primitive interior of an uncivilized continent (Africa) and back home again. Conrad does not name the Congo River or the Belgian Congo region of Africa nor does he identify Africa itself, but he infers by details of travel and geography, that the river which carries Marlow's steamer to Kurtz station is indeed the Congo, and that the continent is Africa. However, Conrad does identify the Thames River and Europe—the river and the continent of the civilized known world. And (b) it is also the story of the conflict between the manager of an ivory company and Kurtz, an ivory agent. The interplay of these two stories constitutes the plot of 'Heart of Darkness' and it is the effect of story No. B on story No. A which carries the theme or unifying principle of the novel.

At the beginning of 'Heart of Darkness' the primary narrator explains that the meanings of Marlow's tales are characteristically difficult to encompass:

> "The yarns of sea-men have a direct simplicity. The whole meaning of which lies within the shell of a cracked nut. But Marlow was not typical (if his

propensity of spin yarns be excepted), and to him the meaning of an episode was not inside like a Kernel but outside, enveloping the tale which brought it out only as a glow brings out a haze, in the likeness of one of those misty halos that sometimes are made visible by the spectral illumination of moonshine."[41]

Conrad's distinction between the usual story and Marlow's uses a metaphor based on contrasted arrangements of two concentric spheres. In the first arrangement, that of the typical seaman's yarn, the direction given our mind is, to use a term from Newtonian Physics, 'centripetal'; the narrative vehicle is the shell, the larger outside sphere which encloses a smaller sphere, the liner kernel of truth; and as readers we are invited to seek this central core of meaning. Marlow's tales, on the other hand, are typically 'centrifugal; the relation of the spheres is reversed; now the narrative vehicle is the smaller inside sphere and its function is merely to reveal a circumambient universe of meanings which are not normally visible and cannot be seen except in association with the story, just as the haze appears only when there is a glow.

'Heart of Darkness', as its name signifies, is the story of a voyage into the very heart of the dark continent Congo in Central Africa. But it is also a journey into the inner darkness, the evil which larks in the heart of men. Its atmosphere of horror, evoked both by the journey without and the journey within, makes it one of the most memorable creations in the language. Based on Conrad's own journey into the dark interior of Central A frica, the story remains upto date, one of the most forceful and outspoken indictment of imperialism and colonial exploitation. It also brings out the maddening horrors, sensations and experience of those who have to face loneliness in more ways than one, and fully deserves the praises that have been showered upon it.

Marlow is the narrator and he narrates the story of his nerve-shattering experience in Congo, 'the heart of darkness', long after his return from Central Africa. It so happens that one day the director of the ivory company, a lawyer, an accountant and Marlow and some others are sitting on the deck of a small ship, the yarn (sailboat) Nellie anchored in the Thames, awaiting the turn of the tide. Marlow, the only one present who still follows the sea.

To this group of listeners, Marlow spins a tale of his only experience with fresh water sailing. He prefaces the story by a reference to ancient times in Britain when:

"This. too, (was once) one of the dark places of the earth."[42]

Home from his sea-faring in the Far East, he was tired of his long vacation and tried to find another ship. Through the influence of an aunt, he secured a job with a company engaged in the ivory trade. Marlow found that everyone in the company office treated him like a doomed person.

He left Europe on a French Steamer. From the time he boarded the ship, his whole adventure took on an unreal dream quality, as though he were voyaging into the regions of fantasy.

The languid sea, the monotonous coastline and his isolation seemed to keep him away from the truth of things. The black men who came out to trade with the ship fascinated and delighted him. They were of real substance, brief contacts with reality.

Marlow left the French ship at the river's mouth and took passage on a river boat commanded by a Swede. The captain's remarks about the government and the country troubled Marlow. The captain related how he took a Swedish compatriot up the river, and the fellow hanged himself. When Marlow asked why, Captain said that the sun was too much for him or the country perhaps.

After a hundred mile trip Marlow landed at the company's outer station and the waste he saw everywhere appalled him. Valuable machinery, tools, and materials lay about in the grass, rusting and broken. A gang of chained black men clanked past him. He turned from the blinding sunlight into a grove of trees and found that it sheltered a throng of dying black workers, animated skeletons, and workout and sickened through labour for the company.

Marlow hurried up the slope to the company buildings and met an astonishing creature—a vision in a high-starched collar, huge white cuffs and elegant clothes. This fashion model proved to be the company's chief accountant, the man who kept the books for the ivory operation. He had been there for three years and his quarters were as neat as his clothing. Everything else about the station was chaotic.

From this man, Marlow first heard of Kurtz. The accountant described Kurtz as a first class agent, a remarkable person in charge of an important station. He sent down more ivory than all the other agents combined. The accountant also confided that Kurtz was in line for a big promotion. He would be somebody in administration before long.

After ten hot and disappointing days at the Outer station, Marlow set out with a caravan of sixty blacks and one white man for the two-hundred-mile trek overland to the Company's Central Station. Each of his carriers had a sixty pound load strapped to his back. The Whiteman proved a poor traveller and had to be carried, thus causing trouble with the carriers. The man was much too heavy.

The trek took fifteen days and Marlow hobbled into the Central Station only to discover that his steamboat was at bottom of the river. His informant said that it would be all right: the manager himself was there and waiting to see him now.

The manager was far from courteous. Although he knew that Marlow had just come two hundred miles over a difficult trail, the manager did not ask him to sit down. He began babbling at once about the wreck. He did not know whether Mr. Kurtz was alive or dead. He estimated that it would take three months to raise the steamer and repair it.

Marlow decided that the manager was a 'chattering idiot' and turned his back on him and the station. He gave his full attention to raising the sunken steamboat. He could not, however, avoid observing the pilgrims—a group of sixteen to twenty white men who carried long staffs and loitered around the station talking about ivory in reverential tones.

One evening a shed full of cheap trade goods caught fire and burned down. Marlow went to look and overheard the manager discussing Kurtz with one of the agents, a hook-nozed fellow with eyes like mica.

Later the brick maker invited Marlow to his room. Marlow marvelled at the elegance of the young agent's quarters-compared with the rest of the station. Marlow thought that the agent must be in favour with the manager and he realised that the agent wanted to pump him, trying to find out about Marlow's influential friends back in Belgium. Marlow did not reveal anything. He let the man believe what he wanted to.

On his way out the door, Marlow saw a small sketch in oils on a panel. It pictured a draped and blind folded woman carrying a lighted torch. The agent explained that Kurtz painted the picture at the Central Station more than a year ago. Marlow questioned him further about Kurtz. He discovered that the agent expected Kurtz to be promoted within a year. He further tells Marlow that Kurtz is a universal genius who finds it difficult to work without all the tools he needs.

One evening Marlow is lying on the deck of his steamboat when he hears two people discussing Kurtz. One of them is upset because Kurtz is so powerful that he can manipulate the company administration in any way he likes. The other man is of the view that the climate would kill Kurtz. But the wonder is that Kurtz is alone at the inner station and still he sends more ivory than all other agents. Reports coming from the interior tell of Kurtz's illness and his imperfect recovery. No one is with him except a lone trader. One man remarks that he had known Kurtz intimately when he was at the station with him, with Kurtz always talking about how each station should be a "beacon on the road towards better things, a centre for trade...humanizing, improving instructions." From this, Marlow concludes that Kurtz is a man of ideals.

Eventually Marlow's vessel is repaired and he starts up river "like travelling back to the earliest beginnings of the world." There is heavy, thick air and heat, vegetation and stillness without peace. Marlow, as captain spends his time trying to keep the boat from sinking, attending to the faulty machinery. He has cannibals for crew and the hippo-meat they brought along, goes rotten and makes 'the mystery of the wilderness stink.' It is the strict routine of keeping his ship afloat and moving which prevents him from running off into the forest to dance with the savages. This continual responsibility maintains Marlow's sanity.

About fifty miles below the Inner Station, Marlow came on an abandoned cabin with a piled stack of wood and a note warning them to "approach cautiously." Here Marlow found a book. It had no cover, but to Marlow it seemed the only real object he had found on the trip. The delays were many, but the manager displayed "a beautiful resignation."

A mile and a half below the Inner Station, an attack took place and the steamer was showered with arrows. A spear thrown through pilot house window fatally wounded the black helmsman. In great fright, the manager ordered Marlow to turn back, but before Marlow could comply with the order, the Inner Station came in sight.

A curiously dressed Russian welcomed them. He proved to be the disciple of Kurtz. He told Marlow that Kurtz was very ill but still alive. The manager and his pilgrims went up to the house to bring Kurtz to the steamer. Marlow talked to the Russian and learnt that Kurtz ordered the attack on the steamer. Kurtz had been without trade goods for many months, yet he had collected ivory at gunpoint until he had a huge supply. He became a god among the natives. They worshipped him and he participated in their horrible secret rites. He had even tried to shoot the Russian who had nursed him through two nearly fatal illnesses.

The men brought Kurtz down to the steamer on an improvised stretcher. He was scarcely more than a cadaver, yet his voice was strong. The shore was filled with natives who did not want their 'deity' to leave. Among them was a magnificent black woman—'savage and superb.'

That night Kurtz escaped and crawled back towards a savage devil ceremony in the jungle. Marlow went after him and brought him back but not before he had glimpsed the vile and 'inconceivable' degradation of the man's soul.

Kurtz entrusted Marlow with a packet of private papers. A few days later Kurtz died with a final cry, 'The horror! The horror!' The next day the pilgrims buried him in a muddy hole.

Afterwards, Marlow became sick and was shipped back to Europe. There, three persons called on him, inquiring about the papers of Kurtz. One was a company officer, another was a musician who claimed to be the cousin of Kurtz and a third was a journalist. Marlow told them that papers of Kurtz were of value and that he was saving them for Kurtz.

Later at her door, Marlow was almost overcome with a vision of the dying Kurtz, his mouth open voraciously as though to devour the whole world. The awful cry 'The horror!' 'The horror!' rang all around him. Marlow entered and met the girl-beautiful, pale and robed in black. She was filled with terrible and deep agony over loss. Her words revealed that she held Kurtz to be the most noble of men-honest, lovable, faithful and true.

For a long time, Marlow answered her evasively. At last, though he said that he had heard last words of Kurtz. She demanded to know them and Marlow lied to the girl. He assured her that her name was the last word on the lips of Kurtz. The girl's loud cry of exultation of "inconceivable triumph and unspeakable pain,' and her subsequent weeping showed Marlow that healing had come at last. By his lie, Marlow freed the girl from her agony and she could now make a healthy recovery. As Marlow left the house, he half-expected the heavens to fall in retribution for his lie—but nothing happened.

The listeners on the deck of the Nellie respond rather insensitively to Marlow's story. The narration of the novel returns to unnamed narrator who describes Marlow as sitting "apart, indistinct and silent in the poise of a meditating Buddha.

The book ends, as it began, with an allusion to Thames:

> "The tranquil water-way leading to the utter most ends of the earth flowed somber under an overcast sky–seemed to lead into the heart of an immense darkness."[43]

Conrad went to Congo in 1890. He reached the outer station at Matadi on June 13 and returned to Europe early the following November. The experiences, recorded in 'Heart of Darkness' occurred between these dates. The manner of his obtaining his appointment, the knitting women and other persons in the Brussels office and the voyage out to Africa are factual. Conrad intended to stay in Congo for three years. He discovered that seven per cent of the company's employees managed to stay that long. Mr. Gosse, a Belgian, was the tailor's model accountant in charge of the outer station. He died six months after Conrad first saw him. The fainting fat man who impeded Conrad's trek to the Central Station had actually come out with him from Brussels. His name was Prosper Herou, a Belgian. The villain of the story, the Central Station manager, was a Belgian named Camille Delcommune. Conrad's account describes his real character.

The steamer was the Roi Des Belges, a fifteen ton boat. The upriver journey began on August 3, covered one thousand miles and consumed twenty-eight days. The Central Station was at Kinchassa, and the Inner station, under the administration of Kurtz, was at Stanley Falls.

The real name of Kurtz was Georges Antoine Klein. He arrived at Congo in 1888; the company appointed him chief of the Inner Station in 1890. His character and that of Kurtz were similar.

Conrad reveals his bitter disappointment over Congo affairs in letters to his aunt, Madame Manguarite Poradowska. He suffered four attacks of fever in two months as well as severe bouts with dysentery. Even the minor incidents in "Heart of Darkness" are mostly factual. Conrad kept a diary of his Congo adventure—the only diary he ever kept.

Critics have discovered many themes in "Heart of Darkness." Some think that Conrad is talking about a man's search for self knowledge. Certainly Marlow had no such conscious goal. Others see a mystical revelation of men's dark self. Still others emphasize Marlow's philosophy that work, faith, and responsibility tend to hold a man in line with civilized standards. All these meanings and many others may rightfully be accepted as threads in the texture of Conrad's most subtle work.

Study of the plot exposes only two lines of aggressive purpose. Marlow develops such a strong purpose to see and talk with Kurtz that it becomes a life and death matter to him.

Since the book closes with a lie which is, in reality, an affirmation of the truth, perhaps Conrad's chief purpose in this story is the discovery and analysis of the double aspects of truth–black truth and white truth, which are both inherent in every human soul. An analysis of the manager's reason for destroying Kurtz shows that at every turn, he works to prevent the truth from being known.

On the opposite side of the struggle, Marlow seeks confirmation of truth. His search is for the 'inner truth'. Like the captain in "The Secret Sharer" who finds his dark self in Leggatt, Marlow finds in Kurtz his own dark self. Throughout the book the black people typify truth and reality. They have ' white souls' while the rapacious whites have black souls.

Conrad also deals in this story with the lure of the abyss—the acrophobia of the soul. The manager and his fellows leap into the abyss, Kurtz is pushed in, while Marlow is drawn to the edge, near enough to 'look over', but habits of integrity, responsibility and a settled faith pull him back. A quote from Charles Dickens in 'A Tale of Two Cities', expresses the truth Marlow discovers:

> "In seasons of pestilence some of us will have a secret attraction to the disease—a terrible passing inclination to die of it. And all of us have like wonders hidden in our breasts, only needing circumstances to evoke them."[44]

In this novel black and white have the usual connotations of evil and good. Throughout the book the white's souls of the black people are contrasted with the black-souled whites who exploit them. The white string of cotton around the starring black boy's neck in the 'grave of death' sets the symbol for the story. The white colours and cuffs worn by the accountant are phony: the man is black with hatred inside. The pale look of the ivory company's manager denotes death. The Bible uses the pale symbol in revelations 6 : 8, the pale "horse" and his rider, "Death." Note that the intended looks pale: she is dying of grief until Marlow 'saves' her with a lie.

The Secret Sharer

Conrad suffered the loss of both parents during his childhood. Sensitive and naturally introspective, he seems never to have escaped his early sadness. Much of his writings deal with a lonely person who for some reason, is cut off from his fellow men. The nameless captain of 'The Secret Sharer' is such a man. He feels himself a stranger among the crew of his ship. When his "other self" appears as the murderer, Leggatt, he is in a frame of mind to accept him. Later, he seems to feel that Leggatt is his own dark self.

Conrad says that the incident he used for 'The Secret Sharer' is true and happened on a vessel cruising in the Far East. He admits that he often saw the captain when he was ashore in English seaport.

Conrad wrote 'The Secret Sharer' in 1909, ten years after "Heart of Darkness." By contrasting the technique in two stories we find how much Conrad learned in ten years from his editors and fellow writers. 'Heart of Darkness' follows the old technique of long sentences, over abundant punctuation and over written paragraphs of ponderous length. Quotes within quotes confuse the reader and long, indefinite words mystify him:

> "A narrow and deserted street in deep shadow, high houses, innumerable windows with venetian blinds, a dead silence, grass sprouting between the stones, imposing carriage archways right and left, immense double doors standing ponderously ajar. I slipped through one of these cracks, went up a swept and ungarnished staircase, as arid as a desert, and opened the first door I came to. Two women, one fat and the other slim, sat on straw-bottomed chairs, knitting black wool. The slim one got up and walked straight at me—still knitting with down-cast eye—and only just as I began to think of getting out of her way, as you would for a somnambulist stood still, and looked up."[45]

"The Secret Sharer" has a modern format. The pages look inviting and all the dialogue is set apart in separate paragraphs. The plot moves along with simple but expressive words and without excessive comments or frequent metaphors.

Many characters Conrad thought necessary to use in "Lord Jim", "Heart of Darkness", and other of his earlier works do not clutter "The Secret Sharer." There are two main characters and only one is named. The psychological plot weaves itself so closely about these two that the few minor characters serve little purpose but to provide background.

The story is told from the point of view of the young, unnamed Captain of the nameless ship; the first person subjective view-point allows the reader into the captain's mind and encourages identifications between protagonist and reader early in the story.

The soul searching nature of the captain's problem makes for frequent passages of exposition and introspection; yet the story moves along in a bright and interesting way. Even the story-within–a story, where Leggatt relates the circumstances of his crime does not confuse the reader nor detract from the story interest.

A nameless ship lies anchored in the gulf of Siam. Her young Captain, also nameless, knows that his crew is tired from the loading operations they have just finished. In order to give them a good night's rest, he offers to omit the anchor watch and stay on deck himself until after midnight. The captain has been in command only a fort-night and feels that his crew still does not fully accept him. His feeling of alienation bothers him. Before the crew turns in, the captain sides another vessel about two miles away. His second mate says the ship is the "Sephora", loaded with coal, a hundred and twenty three days out of Cardiff.

Later in the evening, his crew asleep, the captain discovers that the ship's rope ladder still hangs over the side. He tries to pull it in and discovers that a naked man is hanging to it. The man introduces to him as Leggatt and confesses that he escaped from the 'Sephora'. He murdered a man several week ago and suffered confinement thereafter, but he managed to escape the "Sephora" and swim to the ship of the young captain.

Even before the captain brings out a pair of pajamas and makes his secret guest comfortable, he feels a strange identity with him. This feeling that Leggatt is his other self persists and increases. He hides the murderer in his own cabin at a fearful risk of discovery and when the Sephora's skipper comes to search the captain's ship for the escaped criminal, the captain exerts fantastic efforts to protect the man.

After a few days, during which his feeling of duality with Leggatt mounts to near madness, the captain decides to allow his guest-his "Secret sharer"—to escape at Koh-ring, an island headland where it will be possible to thrust his ship in close enough to shore for a swimmer to reach land.

His crew thinks he is mad and that he is taking the vessel to certain destruction. The captain, however, handles his ship with such skill that he accomplishes his purpose of delivering his 'Secret Sharer' and, at the same time, he elevates himself in the respect of his crew to the position he should occupy.

Both men strike out towards new destinies. Conrad wrote these two works," Heart of Darkness and "The Secret Sharer," about the encounter with one's 'dark self'. The first one he wrote in 1899—a subtle and profound exploration of the subject through recounting his own adventures in Congo. Conrad hid his meanings and challenged his readers to find them. Some of us have found rich treasure in the book, but many others seemed unable to grasp the deep significance of what Conrad intended to communicate.

One suspects that after ten years Conrad heard comment about his "Heart of Darkness" to realize that in order to reach the common mind with his important message, he must present it in a less subtle manner. Perhaps this is the reason why he wrote a much simpler novel which bears essentially the same message.

In both the novels the hero discovers a wicked person for whom he develops an irresistible attraction. In "Heart of Darkness", Marlow is so eager to see and talk with Kurtz that he panics when he thinks he will never reach his goal. In "The Secret Sharer", the captain is so drawn to the murderer, Liggatt, that his mind all but gives way under the strain of obsession for his 'darkself'. In both the novels the hero, who is a good person, identify so fully with evil in the person of a murderer, that the two men almost become one, at least to the hero. Thus they personify the potential for evil which co-exists in every man along with a potential for good.

Both stories happen in connection with ship voyage. The ship signifies the ship of life, and any man's voyage through life may meet such adventures of the spirit.

Both the novels end with deliverance for the hero. "Heart of Darkness" depicts a 'dark-self' (Kurtz) who dies as a god-like hero to the natives. "The Secret Sharer" shows Leggatt, who symbolizes the captain's black soul, as he swims ashore at Koh-ring, delivered from death to seek a new destiny.

In both the novels the white soul undergoes terrible suffering and danger in the final disposition of its black soul. Marlow looks into the abyss in his struggle with Kurtz in the forest just three hundred yards from the pagan convocation which hungers to adore Kurtz as a god. The captain suffers his final conflict as he thrusts his ship closer and closer to the over hanging rock of Koh-ring, risking violent death for himself and his crew.

Through pity and kindness, Marlow subdues Kurtz and carries him back to his couch. Guided by the symbol of his pity (the white hat) for the erring humanity of his 'dark self', the captain releases his secret guest and swings his vessel back into safe channels.

The entirety of "The Secret Sharer" is symbolic. The captain symbolizes every-man. The ship symbolizes everyman's ship of life.

The murderer, Leggatt, symbolizes every man's 'dark-self'.

Prof Ian Watt of Stanford University presents the symbolism and impressionism of "Heart of Darkness" in the following manner:

> "In so far as any specific feature of symbolist literature can be identified, it is more probably the centrifugal way in which the meaning of the work as a whole is conceived."

Such is the final effect of Conrad's title. Compared with the particularity of Conrad's earlier and more traditional titles such as "Almayer's Folly" and "The Nigger of the Narcissus", "Heart of Darkness" strikes a very special note; we are somehow impelled to see the title as much more than a combination of two stock metaphors of referring to 'the Centre of Dark Continent and a diabolically evil person'. Both the nouns are too densely charged with physical and moral suggestion; and together they generate a puzzle which compels us to expect something beyond our usual moral and literary experience; the words do not name what we know, but ask us to know what he has, as yet, no name. The more concrete of the two terms, 'heart', is attributed a strategic centrality within a formless and infinite abstraction, 'darkness'; the combination defies both visualization and logic. How can something inorganic like darkness have an organic centre of life and feeling? How can a shapeless absence of light compact itself into a formed and pulsing presence? And what are we to make of a 'bad' one like darkness? 'Heart of Darkness' was a fateful event in the history of fiction; and to announce it Conrad had hit upon as haunting, though not as obtrusive, an oxymoron as Baudelaire had for poetry with Les Fleurs du Mal".[46]

In this novel the jungle symbolizes truth and reality. Grass is referred to in many places. Grass grows up through Fresleven's skeleton. The meaning of grass symbolism is probably that of the scripture—" ...they are like the grass; In the morning, it flourisheth; in the evening, it is cut down and withereth."[47]

In other words, Conrad wants to say that man's wickedness, as well as their goodness, is transient. Like grass it springs and fades.

"Blinding sunshine" referred to in many places symbolizes the pitiless persecution taking place under the guise of enlightenment.

"The huge buzzing flies" stabbing the dying agent in the accountant's immaculate office symbolize, in general, the operations of the ivory company's representatives—specially the pilgrims. They also symbolize Marlow's reaction to Congo conditions. "The pail with a hole in it" which the fat agent uses to fight the fire symbolizes the inadequacy of all the pilgrims and hangers-on at the central station. Candles symbolize light-feeble light.

'The oil painting' proves that Kurtz understands the situation at the central station, that he knows how stupid and blind the company representatives are and he plunges into darkness and degradation with his eyes open. In this way 'shoes' are mentioned often enough that we wonder what they signify. Marlow flings his bloody shoes into the river. The Russian begs Marlow for a pair of shoes. The packet of papers of Kurtz is tied with a shoe string. According to me they symbolize protection, or guidance or both.

I agree with Edward W. Said, " I do not think it is incorrect to understand the peculiar genius of Conradian narrative specially in such standard setting."[48]

The Nigger of the Narcissus

This work is a story of one of the voyages of the ship, named Narcissus from Bombay to London. The Nigger of the Narcissus is James Wait, a negro who is dying of consumption. During the course of the voyage there is a terrible storm. It is this storm which saves the situation. The men again pull together in their effort to defeat their common enemy, the sea. At the height of the tempest, Mr. Baker, the first mate, asks the cook to make a hot drink. The cook at first too busy is talking about the life to come. Mr. Baker says he will prepare the drink himself, but the cook cannot permit this. He goes towards his wrecked kitchen, shouting:

> "As long as she swims I will cook. The cook finds his stove, 'reared up on end' and is forced, the crew think, to use bread board for a raft."[49]

Even so, at the risk of life, he achieves the apparently impossible task of preparing the drink and puts fresh heart into the weary men. After burying James Wait at the sea, they reach home showing that it is the men and the ship, which matter.

The story is thus a well-told yarn. The Nigger is more than a yarn of the sea. Conrad's concern is with the mental and physical health of the whole crew in the face of the forces which threaten to poison their combined action.

Commenting on the greatness of the novel, Richard Curle writes: "It is impossible to say much about 'The Nigger of the Narcissus' because it is still more a novel without a plot than 'Vanity Fair' is a novel without a hero. And yet it is one of Conrad's most original conceptions. He alone has ever written such a book. It has the vividness of an actual experience touched by the magic glitter of remembrance. The descriptions of the sea and of the life on-board are strangely beautiful. 'The Nigger of the Narcissus' has the qualities of an epic—an epic of the ardous, the exacting, and the enslaving service of the sea."[50]

In a letter to John Galsworthy, dated 17th April, 1899, Joseph Conrad observed:

> "Every word is an object to be considered anxiously with heart searching's and in a spirit of severe resolution."[51]

These words, expressing the author's attitude towards the craft of fiction, provide a motto for all textual scholars editing Conrad texts.

David Leon Higdon, an associate professor of Texas Tech University and joint general Editor of 'Conradiana' says:

> "Indeed, from his very uniqueness as stylist and as fastidious craftsman stem many of the most challenging problems facing those who would give his works the careful attention they need and so richly deserve. Here is the observation based upon strenuous work with the texts of "The Nigger of the Narcissus" and "Almayer's Folly."

Had Conrad been less the painstaking craftsman, seemingly compelled to revise his novels constantly to achieve the effects he desired, editing his work would be an easier task. In his pioneering study, 'Joseph Conrad: The Making of Novelist', John. D. Gordan demonstrated that Conrad time after time reworked his texts. Our work with the holograph manuscript of 'The Nigger', and the fragmentary typescript of the novel prepared by Mrs. Jessie Conrad, confirms Gordan's observations. While suggesting that the author's revisions were more extensive than Gordan demonstrated, a view confirmed by a collection of the printed editions and the copies Conrad marked for revision. Indeed, the text of the novel frequently poses the problem not of whether to admit an amendation but which amendations should finally be included. In the case of 'The Nigger', collation of the printed texts reveals that the early copyright edition (London: William Heinemann, 1897) most closely reflects the state of the holograph and type-script. The serial version in 'The New Review' contains abundant evidence that Conrad revised chapters III-V of that text, while the first British and American editions evidence prove that the author made another separate revision prior to their publication; later Conrad grudgingly bowdlerized proofs of the Heinemann text. Conrad soon revised two of the early printed texts.

It would be tempting in the case of 'The Nigger of Narcissus' to use the hand-marked 1910 Heinemann edition as our copy text. However, the fact that Conrad over looked his earlier substantive revisions, coupled with abundant evidence of compositorial and/or editorial intervention in the accidentals of that edition, complicates the matter...[52]

The following readings indicate the types of problems one encounters. In the holograph manuscript, when the cook approached James Wait's cabin, Conrad had written:

> "He was delighted, frightened, exalted—like on that evening when (the only time in his life-thirty seven years ago, he loved to recall the number of years) when as a young man he had through keeping bad company-become intoxicated in East-end music Hall."[53]

The passage occurs in this form on page 95 of the fragmentary typescript. However, all of the printed editions appearing in 1897 differ. The copyright edition preserves the passage with slight alteration, eliminating the conjunction 'when' near the beginning of the sentence. When the same passage appeared in The New Review, additional alterations are also found.[54]

The substitution of 'as' for 'like' in the sentence may indicate the hand of an editor at work; similarly, the introduction of commas, setting off the phrase 'as a young man' typifies the variant punctuation that sets the serial edition off from other editions:

> "The editors of The Nigger then confront a group of puzzling variants. There is always the possibility that all of these changes may reflect Conrad's intervention, or that none do. Internal evidence supports the arguments that Conrad did revise proofs of chapter III-V of the novel for the New Review. He also prepared copy for the collected editions of the novel, read proofs for Doubleday, and was closely engaged in the editing of the Heinemann collected Edition. In the absence of marked proofs or type-scripts for the later editions or correspondence indicating that the author wished to make such change, inference and taste must play their parts in the editorial judgement."[55]

Nostromo

In a letter on 16th March, 1902 Conrad indicated that he was ready to transmit a 'considerable batch of Nostromo', a 'first rate story' which he felt would eventually run to 75-80,000 words. Conrad apparently expected a good deal financially from Nostromo, for the theme of 'recuperation', as a consequence of the book runs through his exchanges with Pinker. On May 3, 1902, however, even as he writes that Nostromo ought to put me right, he has thoroughly misjudged his progress. For in the same passage, he indicates that the end of the novel is near. This may have been a way of confronting Pinker, whose outlays were increasing, or, more likely, Conrad's own misjudgement of the length of his work.

But 'Nostromo' is another great novel of Conrad. It is based on the history of a South American Revolution. In the Republic of Costaguana, in South America, there is one prosperous and contented province, whose capital Sulaco is the headquarters of the famous 'Gould Company', owners of the Sam Tome silver mine, which has brought about wealth and security to the whole district. The head of the company is an English Costaguana, Charles Gould—a reserved man, hiding in his silence, an inherited love of order and hatred of political unrest that make of him a formidable type of fanatic. His wife, the frail and compassionate Dona Emila is the most moving figure in the whole of Conrad's books. The slow decay of Charles Gould's love of her in his intense absorption in silver is a tragic undercurrent to the story of visible terror and anarchy. For the wealth of Sulaco has attracted, at last, the politicians from beyond the mountains and all the vilest characters of the Republic. In an attempt to upset the reign of the humane president Dictator Ribiera, the one hope of Costaguana, a wild rush is made for Sulaco, both from the mountains and the sea. The whole social fabric, built up with such care falls to pieces at the breadth of revolution. The Sulaco aristocracy, powerless in the hands of a mob who fickle and cringing to the successful, welcome, the victorious revolutionaries with orgies of disorder and joy, await exile and shameful death. But in that gloom and horror is born a new and great idea of the province, that it should be a Republic. It is the idea of the young Decoud, a journalist. His plan is that the province should cut itself off from the rest of the Costaguana and declare itself a Republic. And, in fact, that is what takes place. For at the height of the terror, when Charles Gould and others are expecting instant death, General Barries, one of the faithful General of the Ribiera regime, returns with his army and drives off the invaders.

Nostromo, who is popularly known as Capataz-de-Cargadores, is the most reliable, the most useful and the most feared man in Sulaco. He is a person of almost boundless vanity and resource, and the revelation of his curious, complex character makes, as it were, one of the foundations of the book. For he is a 'man suffering from a grievance which he never reveals—a grievance against society he takes too much for granted, that cheats him of his reward, that cannot adequately recognise all that he has done for it. On the night before the invasion of Sulaco, he is asked to remove the silver treasure out to sea. This voyage of his, with Decoud who is fleeing for his life, is one of the most wonderful things in Conrad. He hides the treasure safely in a desert island, but he never reveals its resting place in anyone else. With Decouds's death and the sinking of the ship, the treasure is supposed to be lost for ever at the bottom of the sea. And Nostromo keeps the secret in his breast and grows rich 'very slowly', visiting the island at night to take away one silver bar after another. And it is there he meets his death by a tragic misunderstanding. For, on the lonely island a lighthouse has been erected now and it is guarded by old Giorgio Viola, and his two daughters, the dark Linda and the fair Gizelle. To Linda, Nostromo, is betrothed but it is Gizelle that he loves. The Garibaldino, knowing nothing of the treasure or of his love, shoot him as he comes to the island one night, thinking he is some other man come on shore to meet his daughter Gizelle.

In the opinion of Richard Curle, 'Nostromo' is Conrad's longest novel and in my opinion it is by far the greatest. It is a book singularly little known and one, which many people find difficult in reading (probably owing to the confused way in which time is indicated), but it is one of the most astounding toure de force in all literature. For sheer creative genius, it overtops all Conrad's works.

As Conrad notified Pinker of these developments and implored patience he was writing paper V of 'The Mirror of the Sea,' while still desperately trying to complete 'Nostromo' which was then well over 100,000 words above his original estimate. His state of mind is recognised when we read in a "Saturday" (May 1904) letter that, he is sending the first batch of Pt III to Pinker. Such desperation has its literary overtones as well, since Conrad evidently saw 'Nostromo' as holding up his entire assembly line of fiction and non-fiction, he was, therefore, particularly anxious to dispose of it. Yet at the same time he writes:

> "I verily believe that 'Nostromo' has elements of success in book form. I've never written anything with so much action in it. The thing is not half bad upon my word."[56]

Nostromo's manner of narration is involved, but its intricacy is highly artistic and the continuity on the whole is convincing. In dramatic vigour, in psychological subtlety, and in the sustained feeling of a mood (an atmosphere at once physical and mental), Nostromo' is a phenomenal masterpiece. It is Conrad's genius incarnate.

Conrad described 'Nostromo' as a story of events flowing from the passions of men short sighted in good and evil. There is in 'Nostromo' an acute awareness of the contradictions in human nature. Conrad knew that men often pretend to be what they are not, or deceive themselves about their real motives, or use for their own advantage the gullibility of others. Conrad often treated these with great scorn.

The Shadow Line

'The Shadow Line' (1917) reverts to the story of Conrad's first command, already recalled in 'The Secret Sharer' and 'Falk'. The story is told autobiographically. The central theme of the hero's first 'ill started command' is introduced by an account of a scheme to prevent him from obtaining it. The tale is neatly framed within a prologue and epilogue. Events follow each other chronologically.

The hero throws up an excellent job; survives an intrigue; reaches his ship as first mate who had himself hoped to become captain, finds his ship calmed, apparently indefinitely, learns gradually the full extent of the late captain's wickedness and madness; sees almost all his crew fall ill; but at last, in a rash, brings the ship safely to port.

"England was at war and 'to sit down and invent fairy tales was impossible' but Norman Sherry, in 'Conrad's Eastern World' has shown how much Conrad added to the original event."[57]

The author declares that he has left some gaps—the last exchanges of the captain with the faithful seaman cannot be loosed to the public's incomprehension.

The young captain begins by suffering from something of the ennui which had seized the diabolic Mr. Jones. Given his first command he goes aboard and confronts his own image in a mirror. At sea, becalmed, with a sick crew and robbed of remedies by the treachery of his predecessor, he takes to a diary; this represents another kind of committal to what "the poet himself, struggling with the form of his coiled work knows."[58]

Conrad says, "I suppose that I did exist on food in the usual way; but the memory is now that in those days life was sustained on an invincible anguish, a sort of infernal stimulant, exciting and consuming at the same time."[59]

A haunted voyage-haunted by the spectre of the dead evil captain—is presented for its effect on the young man. Conrad did not succeed any such sinister being when he took over the otago in 1888 at Bangkok; not all his crew, but three members only, went down with cholera, (the disease that in 1880 had killed Lowry's grandfather in the Indian Ocean, incidentally). 'The work must, therefore, be compared with something as inward as 'Through the Panama'. Otherwise its transformation of the past is too radical for Conrad's claims of exact-truth.

All is done with a fine hold on reality which owes a great deal to the descriptions of the routine-tasks of shipboard. The tale, therefore, contains itself within bounds of complete credibility. The sentences are short, matching the economy of incidents, and the conversation briskly sensible.

The story has a natural rhythm, opening very slowly, picking up as the new Captain goes to take charge of his ship, slowing down to the fixity of a bad dream during the long becalming and then, after the sudden drama of 'the darkness turning into water', moving with energy as the breeze blows.

Conrad's most well known sea-novels have been discussed in this chapter. There are some others too—'Almayer's Folly', 'Arrow of the Gold', 'The Inheritors' (with Ford), 'Nature of a Crime', 'The Mirror of the Sea', 'An Outcast of the Islands etc.

References

1. Conrad Joseph, "A personal Record" Dent Collected Edition, p. 30.
2. In the year of Conrad's death, another pole, Waldyslaw Reymont, won the Nobel Prize for literature. Conrad was, however, offered a knighthood by the Prime Minister in 1924, an honour.
3. William. K. Wimsatt, Jr and Cleanth Brooks, Yale University; Literary criticism, A short History, Oxford and IBH publishing Co. Pvt. Ltd. New Delhi. p. 682-683.
4. Edward W. Said, Conrad and Nietzsche; Edited by Norman Sherry, published by the Macmillan press Ltd, London and Basingstoke, Printed in Great Britain, Reprinted in 1979; p. 66.

5. Conrad, Joseph, 'The Typhoon', Mayoor Paperbacks, published in 1987, p. 3.
6. Eliot T.S., 'The Function of Criticism', 1923, in selected Essays, 1932, 'Tradition and the Individual Talent' in the 'Sacred Wood', 1920.
7. Lowry, Malcomn, Selected Letters, The Macmillan press Ltd, 1980, London, p. 339.
8. M.C. Bradbrook, Narrative form in Conrad and Lowry, (Joseph Conrad, A Commemoration) Macmillan Press, London, Published, 1979, p. 130.
9. James, Henry, 'The New Novel', appeared in Notes on Novelists, 1914.
10. Lowry, Malcolmn, 'Ultramarine', published in 1933 nine years after the death of Conrad.
11. Selected Poems of Malcolmn Lowry p. 74, published by Margery Lowry, 1962, reprinted by Lity Lights Books, London.
12. Conrad, Joseph, "Life and letters" II, p. 155.
13. Eloise Knapp Hay, Political Novels of Joseph Conrad, p. 53; Mayoor paperbacks, New Delhi publication.
14. Long, William J., English Literature (its History and its significance); For the Life of the English speaking world; (Enlarged Edition), Kalyani publishers, New Delhi, Reprint 1989, p. 585-586.
15. Letter to Kane, 12th November 1919, Joseph Conrad, 'To my Brethren of the pen', (privately Printed), p. 1, Taken from Rhetoric and Ideology in Conrad's 'Western Eyes' First Para.
16. 'The Nigger of the Narcissus', (London, Dent 1950) Dent's collected edition in 21 volumes.
17. "The structures of Fiction" Modern languages Notes 84 (1969), p. 891-915; and "Novel and Narrative", in the Theory of the Novel, ed. John Halperin, (New York, 1974) p. 155-174.
18. Andrzej, Busza, (Rhetoric and Ideology in Conrad's 'Western Eyes' from Joseph Conrad; A Commemoration, The Macmillan Press Ltd, 1979; Gilbert Phelps in the 'Russian Novel in English Fiction', London, 1956, p. 54.
19. Eliot, George, Silas Mariner, The Heritage of literature, series section B No 46; pp. part two 159-60, 220.
20. Conrad, Joseph, 'Typhoon', Surjeet Publication, p. 43-44.
21. Conrad, Joseph, 'Lord Jim,' Mayoor classic series; Pub-1987, p. 5-6.
22. Kocowna, Barbora, 'The problem of language'. The Macmillan press Ltd, 1979, p. 194-196.
23. Kocowna Barbara, Joseph Conrad: A Commemoration, The Macmillan press Ltd, London, 1979, p. 196.
24. Kocowna, Barbara, The Problem of Language, The Macmillan press, pub. 1979, p. 196-197.
25. *Ibid.*, p. 197.
26. Leavis, F.R., The Common Pursuit, Chats and Windus, London, 1954, p. 193 and 261.

27. Richard Curle, Joseph Conrad: A Study (London: Kegan Paul, French, Tribner and Co. 1914).
28. Conrad, Joseph, 'Lord Jim', Mayoor Classic Series, India. First Mayoor Edition, 1989, p. 7-8.
29. *Ibid.,* p. 11.
30. *Ibid.,* p. 22.
31. *Ibid.,* p. 131.
32. *Ibid.,* p. 132.
33. *Ibid.,* p. 204.
34. *Ibid.,* p. 224-225.
35. *Ibid.,* p. 227-228.
36. *Ibid.,* p. 228.
37. *Ibid.,* p. 231.
38. *Ibid.,* p. 233.
39. *Ibid.,* p. 246-247.
40. George. Jean Aubry, Joseph Conrad. 'Life and Letters',(Garden city): Doubleday, Doran, 1927, p. 276.
41. Conrad, Joseph, 'Heart of Darkness', Mayoor paperbacks, Noida, India, p. 48.
42. *Ibid.,* p. 8.
43. *Ibid.,* last paragraph.
44. Dickens, Charles, 'A Tale of Two Cities'.
45. Conrad, Joseph, 'Heart of Darkness', Mayoor Paperbacks Classics, Noida 1986, p. 55-8.
46. Watt, Ian, "Impressionism and Symbolism in 'Heart of Darkness', The Macmillan press Ltd, (a paper from 1914 International conference on Conrad) published 1979 (Last Para), p. 53.
47. The Bible: Psalm 90.
48. Conrad and Niethche, p. 69.
49. Conrad, Joseph, 'The Nigger of Narcissus', Mayoor Paperbacks, Noida, p. 53.
50. Curle, Richard, 'Joseph Conrad: A Commemoration.' The Macmillan press Ltd, printed in Great Britain. by Unwin Brothers Ltd, London, 1979, p. 190.
51. Georges, Jean Aubry, 'Joseph Conrad: 'Life and Letters' (Garden City, Doubleday, Doran, p. 276.
52. Higdon, David Leon, On Editing Conrad, The Macmillan press Ltd. London, 1979, p. 143-144.
53. 'The Nigger of the Narcissus', Holograph Manuscript, p. 124.
54. Conrad. Joseph, 'The Nigger of the Narcissus'. The New Review, XVIII. (November,. 1897) p. 493.
55. Kenneth, W. Davis, Joseph Conrad: A Commemoration, The Macmillan press Ltd, 1979, p. 149.
56. Letter of Conrad to James Brand Pinker. his literary agent from 1899-1922.

57. Norman sherry, Prof. of English literature, University of Lancaster. 'Narrative Form in Conrad and Lowry', The Macmillan press Ltd, London, 1979, p. 146.
58. The epigraph is from Baudelaire, La Musique D'autre fois, Calme plat, grand miroir Detman desepoir.
59. Cf. Joseph Conrad, A Personal Record, p. 100. The passage in which Conrad describes the dream-state of anguish in which he worked at Nostromo is the nearest reflection of the captain's mood.

5

Impressionism in Conrad

> "It was not important that things be beautiful (for the impressionist); what he sought to discover was their identity—the signs by which he should know them."
>
> —Henry James ("A New England Winter")

Impressionism, a magic word that conjures visions of the fresh, true and beautiful in fact, has come to bear meanings it did not possess for writers and painters when the movement was alive. For Conrad, as for Henry James, impressionism was very different from what it became, for instance, in 1932 when Joseph Warren Beach classified Conrad as an impressionist. While both Conrad and James would have accepted the Impressionist Painter's principle that a true artist deals only with accurate sense of perception, rejecting academic rules and fixed conceptions, both novelists found the impressionist painters and writers who followed them to be deficient in one important respect; they rejected depth analysis and the probing of hidden human mysteries.

Ford Madox Ford was wrong, then, when he claimed after Conrad's death that the novelist "accepted the stigma of "Impressionist."[1] More accurately, Ford claimed in 1914 that certain "maxims" which he called impressionism had been "gained mostly in conversation with Mr. Conrad."[2] Readrs see Conrad's hand and hear his voice in these maxims, but it is hard to reconcile Ford's use of the word 'impressionism' with Conrad's decisive use of the term.

One answer to the riddle would be to consider that in addition to French impressionism, which Conrad ridiculed, there was an older English movement that rarely went by the name. Through the criticism of Walter Peter, Conrad and James became sympathetic with this tradition. Further, light is thrown by discovering possible link, missing between Ford's "maxims" and Conrad's unkind words about impressionism. 'The missing link might be found in an essay, the title of which is 'Impressionism in the Novel', by Brunetiere in 1879.[3]

The essay of Ferdinand was a searching review of Alphonse Daudet. In Conrad's later essay on Daudet in 1898, he treated Daudet much as he treated Crane—as a wonderful secondary writer with a gift for seeing, only the surface of things… for the reason that most things have nothing but a surface"[4]—a remark that paraphrases another famous critic of impressionism, Paul Gauguin.

We find three clear phases in the attitude of Conrad regarding impressionism; the first in his disgust at a collection of impressionist paintings in 1891; the second when he met Crane and gave qualified praise to his art in 1897, soon afterwards writing his Preface of 'The Nigger of the Narcissus', and the third at the end of his life when he curiously reversed himself after years of denigrating the movement and began to aim the same effects that he had earlier questioned.

Let us see what Eloise Knapp Hay says "Conrad undoubtedly read Brunetiere before reading Peter. Brunetiere was Marguerite Poradowska's editor at La Revue des seus Mondes, in the early 1890s while she—Tante Margot—was Conrad's only literary confident. Joseph Conrad mentions him twice in letters to her (later also in "A Personal Record." chapter 5) and speaks of himself as a member of Brunetier's 'Daudet Cult.' If Conrad read Brunentier's essay on Daudet and impressionism, he probably did so after 1883, when it made one chapter in a book of Brunetier's titled 'Naturalism in the Novel.' Like Zola before him, Brunetiere saw impressionism as one sort of naturalism, and indeed the painters saw themselves as naturalists, Bruntiere commends the impressionists for rejecting Zola's squalid vision; also for correcting Flaubert (progenitor of naturalism) in his "disdainful impassivity" as between author and characters. Nearly echoing Brunetiere, Conrad at different times said he never sought in art anything but 'a form of the beautiful.'[5]

Conrad's method as between authors and characters is "aimed essentially at the intimacy of a personal communication".[6]

For Brunetiere the main attraction of Daudet's impressionism was that it was able "before all to open our eyes to see the distinctive trait, to accustom our hands to rendering the primal aspect of things for the eyes of others… that is the first point."[7]

It was also the most important point in Conrad's preface to 'The Nigger of the Narcissus'.

There were other 'truths' that Brunetiere found among the errors of impressionism. He praised the power of impressionist to present the raw data of chaotic experience and then make sense out of it. Meaning is not imposed on experience but found in it. One finds examples of this everywhere in Joseph Conrad. For instance in Marlow's gradual reading of incomprehensible sensations after Fudea explodes.[8]

Brunetiere says that the impressionist does not create characters, he encounters them—again a maxim of Ford's impressionism. Conrad's ambiguous narrator, mingling alternately with crew and officers of the Narcissus, achieved this effect; also the other one Brunetiere demanded of counteracting Flaubert's impassivity. Conrad's narrator lives and suffers with his characters. As Ford said in 1924, "life does not narrate but makes impressions on our brains."[9]

Brunetiere remarks that Daudet and the literary impressionists often suppress parts of speech normally demanded by logic or convention. The lost connectives in conversation—so loved by James and Ford—are examples of this, as are the lost syntactical references that have been found trouble-some in Conrad's writing.[10] Ian Watt, commenting on this in a letter to Eloise Knapp Hay of June 18, 1974, writes of one puzzling passage:

> "Conrad was thinking in terms larger and more subjective than his syntax allows."[11]

In 'Under Western Eyes', Razumov's eye falls on the statue of a running youth, just as Haldin's escape and his own threatened life confront him as irreconcilable. The emphasis is a telling example of Conrad's labours in this method, as is Kurtz's allegorical painting. Conrad seemed to envy Stephen Crane, his power to express human experience purely as sensation in the first lines of 'The Open Boat': "None of them knew the colour of the sky."[12]

In this way one could invent Brunetiere from Ford's maxims for impressionism. What one cannot find in Ford is that Bruntiere and Conrad after him had almost as much to say against the "errors" of impressionism as for its "truth". Brunetiere saw impressionism as one more manifestation of the tendency in modern literature to substitute physical sensation for inward experience. He points out:

"It is no longer literature if language forces itself to evoke not the ideas of things but they think themselves."[13]

The spectre of Butler's 'Chosisme' is already taking shape. Conrad seems also to confront it when he speaks of his concern with 'les valeurs ideales.' He said that his art depended on "unconventional grouping and perspective", these methods of forcing the reader to look deeply into things.[14] Conrad's whole relation to impressionist movement on Brunetiere's final trade is against it. The great writers in all times Brunetiere says, "did not play at being artists, or dilettantes of the undulating... surfaces of things; they went straight to the bottom of things first."[15]

Out of three phases of Conrad's view point towards impressionism the first phase begins appropriately with his reactions to impressionist painters. He was related to a minor impressionist painter, Paul VanRyssel, as the painter called himself. In real life he was the medical doctor Paul Gachet, blood cousin of Marguerite Gachet Poradowska. In 1890 Van Gogh died virtually in Gachet's arm. Next year in Paris Conrad visited Madame Poradowska and found her walls hung with a superb collection of impressionist paintings. She was staying in Gachet's apartment, and he had acquired them during the twenty previous years, out of charity for his unsolvable fellow painters. When his collection was given to the Louvre in the 1950's it included paintings by Monet, Renoir, Picasso, Sisley, Van Gogh, and Cezanne. After seeing these paintings, Conrad returned to London and wrote to his Cousin:

> "I don't like to think of you in Doctor's apartment. It is too nightmarish with that collection of paintings by the School of Charenton."[16]

'Charenton' meant, of course, the school of madmen, like the Marquis de Sade and Van Gogh.

In 1876 Henry James reviewed the second Impressionist Exhibition in Paris for the New York Tribune. Calling the painters 'the irreconcilables' he wrote:

> "the effect was to make me think better than ever of all the good old rules which decree that beauty is beauty and ugliness is ugliness... The Impressionists are partisons of unadorned reality and absolute foes to arrangement, embellishment, selection...Let (beauty) alone, they say, and it will come at its own pleasure; the painters proper field is simply the actual and to give a vivid impression of how a thing happens to look, at a particular moment."

Two years later James argued that:

> "A picture is not an impression but an expression—just as a poem or a piece of music is."[18]

But within four years, James wrote in 'The Art of Fiction': "The novel is in its broadest sense, a direct impression of life." The novel's value, he added, is greater or less according to the intensity of the impression. Conrad's evolution followed a similar course, beginning fifteen years later than James's. After initial revulsion, Conrad wrote his quasi-impressionist Preface to 'The Nigger' in 1898. He refused to connect himself with any isms. Conrad here, nevertheless, defined all arts as an impression conveyed through the senses:

> "A work that aspires, however humbly, to the condition of art should carry its justification in every line. And art itself may be defined as a single-minded attempt to render the highest kind of justice to the visible universe, by bringing to the light the truth, manifold and one, underlying its every aspect. It is an attempt to find in its forms, in its colours, in its light, in its shadows, in the aspect of matter and in the facts of life, what of each is fundamental, what is enduring and essential—their one illuminating and convincing quality—the very truth of their existence. The artist, then, like the thinker or the scientist, seeks the truth and makes his appeal. Impressed by the aspect of the world, the thinker plunges into ideas, the scientist into facts-whence, presently, emerging they make their appeal."[19]

The preface betrays a bias, again like James's, against the breezy surface effects and rejection of chiaroscuro in impressionistic painting—and with some justice, since the painters themselves declared it their purpose to study the effects of light on surfaces repudiating the Academy's stress on sculptural plasticity's. Perhaps pointedly, Conrad's Preface twice mentions that fiction must have not only the colour of painting and the magic suggestiveness of music but also the plasticity of sculpture. In fact Like Conrad at this time, the post impressionist painters from Seurat and Cezanne through Picasso were all trying to discover the stillness, solidities, depths and multiple perspectives that the impressionists rather deliberately foreswore. Conrad's view in this second phase of his attitude toward impressionism is clear from what he said about Stephen Crane.

Conrad said that it was Edward Gernett, in an article of 1898, which recognised Crane as 'chief of the impressionists.' Garnett's essay owes nothing to Brunetiere. It reflects rather what Mallarme had written in 1876 about the French painters. "Their results appear to have been attained at the first stroke… that which I preserve through the power of impressionism is the power of having recreated nature touch by touch. I leave the massive and tangible solidity to its fitter exponent sculpture. I content myself with reflecting on the clear and durable mirror of painting, that which perpetually lives yet dies every moment."

Similarly Garnett wrote of Crane:

> "We would define him by saying he is the perfect artist and interpreter of the surfaces of life… To dive into hidden life is, of course, for the artist a great temptation and a great danger…the artist seeking to interpret life, departs from the truths of nature."[20]

Conrad, in his second phase, did not go so far as Garnett in admiring Crane. In 1897, he wrote to Garnett:

> "Crane's thought is concise, connected, never very deep—yet often starling. He is the only impressionist and only an impressionist."[21]

That Conrad did not consider himself an impressionist, as Beach claimed, was still clear in 1900 when Conrad wrote thanking R.B. Cunninghame Graham for a book of stories:

> "they are much more than mere Crane like Impressionism but even as impressionism these sketches are well nigh perfect."[22]

Conrad thus moved from a phase of despising impressionism as a school of madmen to recognising it as an appealing, superficial movement in the arts, a style that gave back pure, bright, surface effects of nature, as in the 'clear durable mirror' of Mallarme. Yet Conrad's letters at this time insist that brilliant surfaces are incapable of capturing what he repeatedly called 'the Inner Truth' or 'flesh and blood' of life. Technical facility could even interfere with truth in art, Conrad held. He wrote to Galsworthy,

> "Technical perfection, unless some real glow to illumine and warm it from within, must necessarily be cold."[23]

And explaining why there seemed to be no 'flesh and blood' in James' fiction, Conrad said that James wrote perhaps with too much perfection of method.

His own labours to fathom experience cost him more than he ever wanted to pay, these same letters show. Gernett might have been thinking of Conrad when he said that the artist seeking to interpret life departs from nature. John Rewald confirms that this was the opinion of impressionist painters:

"Nature (for them) was no longer an object susceptible of interpretation: it became the direct source of pure sensations."[24]

From 1898 until Conrad wrote 'The Rover', he saw an important half-truth in this doctrine, but never a whole truth. He wished to collaborate with Crane in 1898, perhaps hoping to steal a bit of his fire without being burned. His reasons for turning then to Ford for collaboration suggest the same search for help in achieving the swift mastery over words, over impressions. With such an ally, he said, he could then 'descend into (his) own little hell for his main work'.[25]

The power in himself that Conrad named insistently was what he called 'analyses. This seems a direct echo from Maupassant's divides modern novelists into those who are objective and those who are 'partisans of analyses. Plainly Maupassant's sympathies are with objective writers (like himself and Flaubert), who render life 'as it is—manifested' under the facts of existence. 'Analysis' was a word often used also by painters who criticized impressionism. Cezanne and Gaygin sought the very thing that Maupassant rejected. As Conrad virtually said of Crane, Cezanne said of Monet, "He is only an eye but, my God, what an eye!"[26]

For Conrad's own struggles with 'analysis', several times mentioned in his letters of October 4, 1906 to Garnett, he offered to shorten 'The Secret Agent', if an editor wished. He writes, "I can take out 2 to 3 thousand words if so desired-analysis".[27]

Cezanne, like Conrad, was determined to seek 'structure beneath richly nuanced surfaces.'[28]

Gaygin too criticized the impressionists this way. He said, "they look for what is near the eye, and not at the mysterious heart of thought."[29]

The same reaction away from objective impressionism was marked by Proust. His objection to the realism of the Goncourts—so similar to Conrad's objection to Arnold Bennett's realism—in Proust's Contre Sainte Beuve (Paris, Gallimard, 1971, p. 642).

Proust reminds us of another aspect of impressionism, important both to him and to Conrad, the quality called 'temperament'. Conrad often spoke of writing as the temperamental handling of personal experience. Rewald points out how important the word 'temperament' was for Baudelaire and Zola. Baudelaite said of Manet "he has temperament that is the important thing."[30]

Zola searched among painters for what he called, "creation seen through the medium of a powerful temperament."[31]

Perhaps struck by these remarks, Peter soon afterwards wrote, "What is important is not a correct abstract definition of beauty for the intellect, but a certain kind of temperament."[32]

Beauty is a response of temperament to certain kinds of impressions. For Pater in 1873, "What is real in our life finds itself down to a single sharp impression."[33]

Conrad's 'preface to The Nigger' connects impression with temperament but then goes on to stress that the artists appeal is always from one temperament to another. Brunetiere also made this point, as cited above. For Conrad, the artist thus achieves two ethical as well as aesthetic results: first, attachment to the earth, which often otherwise seems alien, and secondly the solidarity of mankind. Conrad adds that the artist's power may extend further still, to give us that 'glimpse of truth' for which the reader has forgotten to ask. Whereas Pater treated the recording of impressions, through temperament, as fully justified by a heightened awareness of life. Conrad redirects the current of this modern Epicurus into stoic's ethic, worthy of Zeno, but modern in its suggestions of man's strangeness in nature.

Pater's impressionism is a necessary supplement to the mainstream of impressionism in France. It is a direct and natural development from seventeenth century English empiricism and the later philosophy of David Hume. In France impressionism represented not a development but a revolt—against the main philosophical tradition of Descartes. French impressionism expressed itself first among painters revolting against the Sacrosanct Academy. The movement, therefore, became associated with lunacy. This was not true in England if one looks at the tradition of Hume, as Ford was minded to do. The word 'impressionism' was coined by John Rogers in 1839, referring to Hume's tradition.

Hume's great question was, "how do I move from the hard facts of sense data to certain knowledge?" The question would make a good second epigraph for 'Lord Jim'. In 1921 Conrad told Louis Lenormand that the great novel still to be written would be about "the decline of men who have reached a sense of certitude."[34]

Hume concluded that man's pursuit of certainty will never be satisfied, but such certainty as is necessary to life could be derived from sense impressions. As the first sentence of his 'Treatise of Human Nature' read, "All perceptions of the human mind resolve themselves into impressions and ideas."

Ideas are poor, second in the pursuit of truth, however, since ideas are only the residue of impressions. Hume established thus that impressions are the generative force behind all knowledge. Pater merely poeticised an 'impressionism' elaborated over a century earlier. It was already accepted when William Hazlitt pronounced, "I think what I feel. I cannot help receiving certain impressions from things and I have sufficient courage to declare... what they are."[35]

The combined force of Hume and Pater, perhaps corrected by Brunetiere, may have moved Conrad towards the near-impressionism of his second phase. The third and last phase of his interest was brief, and marked by a curious reversal of his earlier stand on Crane's impressionism. In 1919, Conrad wrote that Crane was "the chief impressionist of our day," acknowledging the phrase as Garnett's. But in 1898, he also wrote, Crane was "never great in the sense of so fusing...a whole that the reader is struck dumb as by an inevitable revelation'. Now, in 1919, Conrad insists contrarily that Crane, 'had a wonderful power of vision... that seemed to reach, within life's appearances and forms, the very spirit of life's truth. To Garnett's argument that Crane was 'the perfect artist and interpreter of the surfaces of life'; Conrad answers, "His impressionism of phrase went really deeper than the surface."[36]

It seems possible that private jokes between Conrad and Garnett about 'Stevie' (as they called Crane) may have come into portrait Conrad drew after Crane's death of Winnie Verloc's half witted brother Stevie, who like Crane had an unusual attachment to horses, a weak lower lip, and an unrestrained temperament. Garnett's perfidy in divulging the joke cause for Conrad's indignation. But, discounting that, Conrad had reasons bearing on his present fiction that would adequately explain the reversal of his early stand on Crane's impressionism.

We know that in writing 'The Rover', Conrad prided himself on at last achieving a novel that was deftly objective and short, a novel from which 'analysis' was absent and all search for 'the truth of life' ended in the palpable 'facts of existence'. A year after publishing 'The Rover', Conrad was more than ever concerned with achieving 'objectivity', similar to the impressionism he once deprecated in Crane but which now, as the essays on Crane show, he considered more than ever desirable.

This was when he met Lenormand in Corsica, while there hoping to capture impressions for the writing of 'Suspense':

"Denying that he wishes to look below the surface of things, he backs away

> from discussion of the deeper meanings of his great novels. 'I am only a story-teller, he says. 'I do not want to go to the bottom of things. I want to consider reality as something rough and crude over which I let my fingers play. Nothing more."[37]

Conrad's remark was instigated by Lenormand's 'discovery' of Freudian meanings in 'Almayer's Folly' and 'Lord Jim'. Psychoanalysis, as then understood, seems to have given Conrad more reason to side with the enemies of 'analyses.

Conrad, perhaps, came to believe it was better not to look too deeply into things, or perhaps, now that impressionism was dead all over Europe, he wanted to praise it. His view of it, as of Stephen Crane, was elegiac; and he was always good at elegies.

Also this change of heart was like nostalgia for his middle years, when literary 'schools' and 'isms' were lively issues, and when he knew, or thought he knew, the great difference between surfaces and what lay beneath.

Instead of photographically presenting sea life and the life of tropical areas with extreme realism, Conrad sought to interpret the sea life and the life of forests and through the colour of his imagination gave the impression of that life. Conrad's success as an impressionist will be analyzed through 'The Heart of Darkness' and 'The Nigger of the Narcissus'. Those qualities of our being that fit us best for the hazardous enterprise of living. They speak authoritatively to our common sense, to our intelligence, to our desire of peace or to our desire of unrest; seldom to our prejudices, sometimes to our fears, often to our egoism—but always to our credulity. And their words are heard with reverence, for their concern is with weighty matters: with the cultivation of our minds and the proper care of our bodies; with the attainment of our ambitions; with the perfection of the means and the glorification of our precious aims. It is otherwise with the artist.

Confronted by the same enigmatical spectacle the artist descends with himself and in that lonely region of stress and strife, if he be deserving and fortunate, he finds the terms of his appeal. His appeal is made to our l ess obvious capacities, to that part of our nature which because of the war like conditions of existence, is necessarily kept out sight within the more resisting and hard qualities—like the vulnerable body within the steel armour. His appeal is less loud, more profound, less distinct, more stirring—and sooner forgotten. Yet its effect endures for ever. The changing wisdom of successive generations discards ideas, questions facts, demolishes theories. But the artist appeals to that part of our being which is not dependent on wisdom: to that in us which is a gift and not an acquisition—and, therefore, permanently enduring. He speaks to our capacity for delight and wonder, to the sense of mystery surrounding our lives; to our sense of pity, and beauty, and pain; to the latent feeling of fellowship with all creation and to the subtle but invincible, conviction of solidarity that knits together the loneliness of innumerable hearts; to the solidarity in dreams, in joy, in sorrow, in aspirations, in illusions, in hope, in fear, which binds men to each other, which binds together all humanity—the dead to the living to the unborn.

It is only some such train of thought, or rather of feeling, that can in a measure explain the aim of the attempt, made in the tale which follows, to present an unfruitful episode in the obscure lives of a few individuals out of all the disregarded multitude of the bewildered, the simple and the voiceless. For, if there is any part of truth in the belief conferred above it becomes evident that there is not a place of splendour or a dark corner of the earth that does not deserve, if only a passing glance of wonder and pity. The motive then, may be held to justify the matter of the work; but this preface which is simply an avowal of endeavour, cannot end here—for the avowal is yet complete.

References

1. Conrad, Joseph, 'A Personal Remembrance' (London, 1924) p. 182—Ford's and Stephen Crane's Impressionism may be related to discussion of the subject, Indexed in Jean Cazemajou's Stephen Crane (Paris, 1969).
2. Hueffer, Madox Ford, 'On Impressionism', in Poetry and Drama (Paris, June and December, 1914), vol. II; p. 167-75 & 323-24.
3. Brunetiere, Ferdinand, 'Impressionism dans le roman', in La revue des deuse mondes; Paris, 15 Nov, 1879; p. 446-59; English translation by Eloise Knapp Hay.
4. Alphonse Daudet, in Notes on Life and Letters (London, 1921); p. 28.
5. Conrad, Joseph, Edited by Norman Sherry; Unwin Brothers Ltd. 1979; p. 55.
6. Conrad's references to Brunetiere are in Letters de Joseph Conrad, a Marguerite Paradowska; edited Reve Rapin p. 157-58. His reference on his own art are in 'A Familiar Preface', and in his Letter to Richard Curle of 14th July, 1923.
7. "Impressionism dans Le roman' in Le roman naturalist; p. 89-90.
8. Brunetiere, loc. cit; Edward Said, Joseph Conrad, The Fiction of Autobiography (Cambridge, Mass, 1966) pp. 107-8; and Ian Watt in a paper delivered at Warsaw in 1972.

9. Ford, Conrad Joseph, 'A Personal Remembrance (London, 1924); p. 18-82.
10. Brunetiere, p. 92.
11. Conrad, Joseph, A Commemoration', Edited by Norman Sherry (Unwin Brothers Ltd., 1979).
12. Stephen Crane, Last Essays (London, Dent 1940); pp. 102-3.
13. Brunetiere, p. 92.
14. Letters of March 18, 1917, to Sidney Colvin; and July 14, 1923 (both in Jean-Aubry, Life and Letters).
15. Brunetiere, p. 104-5.
16. Letters de Joseph Conrad a Morguerite Poradowska; p. 87 (Translated from French by Eloise Knapp Hay).
17. James Henry, 'The Impressionists' in 'The Painters' Eye', Ed J.L. Sweeney (New York, 1956); p. 114-15.
18. 'The Painters' Eye', p. 28.
19. Quoted in John Rewald. 'The History of Impressionism. (New York, 1973) p. 372-74.
20. Garnett Edward, 'Friday Night' (London, 1922), p. 206.
21. Letter of 5th December, 1897 to Garnett (Letters from Joseph Conrad, Indian Podis 1928) p. 119.
22. Joseph Conrad's Letters to R. B. Cunninghame Graham ed. C.T. Watts (Cambridge, England, 1969) p. 119.
23. Letters to Galsworthy, 'Life and Letters, 1; pp. 270-71.
24. Rewald; pp. 284 & 330.
25. Letter of October, 1898, to W.E. Henley, quoted in Braines's Joseph Conrad (London, 1959); pp. 217-19.
26. A Dictionary of Art and Artists (London, 1960); p. 277.
27. *Ibid.*
28. Rewald, p. 558.
29. Rewald, pp. 574-575.
30. Letter to Madame Paul Maurice of 24th May 1865, quoted in Rewald in p. 54.
31. From an essay of Zola on Proudhan, quoted in Rewald in p. 143.
32. Pater, 'Preface to the Renaissance'
33. Conclusion to the Renaissance.
34. Lenormand Louis, 'Note sur un sejour le Conrad en Corse', in La nouvelle nevue franchise; XXIII (December, 1924) p. 670; English translation by Eloise Knapp Hay.
35. Hazlitt, William, Preface to 'A View of the English Stage' (1818), in works (London, 1930-34), V. 175.
36. 'Stephen Crane' reprinted in 'Notes on Life and Letters', p. 50.
37. Lenormand, p. 69 translation by Eloise Knapp Hay.

6

Conradian Voice

The work of Joseph Conrad is relevant today because it was produced in the simpler Europe which existed before 1914. It was written in the presence of general standards of public sanity to which we never returned in the post-war years, yet by the peculiar history of his country, his family and himself, Conrad knew horrors almost equal with those of today and in this particularly commanding position he was fitted to be an example of a good European—a type which belongs not to the past but to the future. In himself, he knew and loved Poland, France and England, he loved England most proudly, France most warmly, Poland most deeply. Conrad's reconciliation of their conflicting claims, and his sympathy with the best of what was common to the three, is his final triumph of reducing the complex to the simple and the one which deserves the gratitude of all.

But the novelist took art seriously and condemned those who take art for art's sake. His aim was not to run away from the realities of life, he was not an escapist, on the other hand, he has presented life as he has seen it. Conrad's approach to literature is an integrated approach in the sense that he responds to the demands of both outer and inner life. Conrad had actually followed consciously or unconsciously the lessons of art as imparted by Maupassant, Flaubert, Henry James and Dostoievski through their works but he was not bound down by any model or dogma. Conrad has explained most elaborately and clearly his artistic creed or conception of art in his preface to his novel, 'The Nigger of the Narcissus', he says that "a work that aspires, however humbly, to the condition of art should carry its justification in every line."[1]

He was against all sorts of artificiality and verbosity although some of the critics have adversely appreciated his vocabulary and his literary expression in most of his sea-tales.

Conrad is much nearer to Flaubert than to any other literary artist in his conception of art. I am presenting how Conrad defines art:

> "Art itself may be defined as a single-minded attempt to render the highest kind of justice to the visible universe, by bringing to light the truth, manifold and one, underlying its every aspect. It is an attempt to find in its forms, in its colours, in its light, in its shadows, in the aspects of matter and in the facts of life what of each is fundamental, what is enduring and essential—their one illuminating and convincing quality—the very truth of their existence. The artist, then like the thinker, or the scientist, seeks the truth and makes his appeal."[2]

So, the ideal or rather the mission of an artist is to see and experience life in order to seek the truth about the world in which we live, and present that truth or those truths to his readers. In the eyes of Conrad, the position of an artist is more like that of a thinker or a scientist who tries to know the fundamentals of life. Of course, the thinker deals in ideas while the scientist deals in facts. According to Conrad, the artist, the thinker and the scientist—all prepare us for the challenges of life, for the risky or dangerous or uncertain enterprise of living. Conrad says that 'the thinker and the scientist speak authoritatively to our common sense, to our intelligence, to our desire of peace or to our desire of unrest, seldom to our prejudices, sometimes to our fears, often to our egotism but always to our credulity. Their words are heard with reverence, for their concern is with the weighty matters, with the cultivation of our minds and the proper care of our bodies, with the attainment of our ambitions, with the perfection of the means and the glorification of our precious aims.'

The artist undoubtedly tries to present the truths of life but in a different way or methods from that of the thinker and the scientist. The artist appeals to our feelings and emotions, to our capacity for delight and wonder, and also to our latent feeling of comradeship with all the creations–men, brides and beasts, rocks, trees and flowers and above all, land, water and the air—which Conrad believed to be the universal tie that links up the living with the non-living. In the case of thinkers and scientists, their ideas and facts are investigated, inquired into, and challenged by all succeeding generations of the human race. But the artist is not challenged unless he presents some false picture of life. Let us see what Conrad says in this connection:

> "Confronted by the same enigmatical spectacle, the artist descends within himself and in that lonely region of stress and strife, if he is deserving and

> fortunate, he finds the terms of his appeal. His nature which, because of the war like conditions of existence, is necessarily kept out of sight, within the more resisting and hard qualities, like the vulnerable body within a steel armour. His appeal is less loud, more profound, less distinct, more stirring and sooner forgotten. Yet its effect endures forever. The changing wisdom, successive generation discards ideas, questions facts, demolishes theories. But the artist appeals to that part of our being which is not dependent on wisdom. He speaks to our capacity for delight and wonder, to the sense of mystery, to the latent feeling of fellowship with all creation and to the subtle but invincible conviction of solidarity that knits together the loneliness of innumerable hearts, to the solidarity in dreams, in joy, in sorrow, in aspirations, in illusions, in hope, in fear, which binds men to each other, which binds all humanity, the dead to the living and living to the unborn."[3]

Certain critics have tried to undermine the reputation of Conrad as a writer by saying that he is an artist of loneliness. Although Conrad has taken lessons from Dickens or Thackeray, Galsworthy or H.G. Wells in the method or conception of his art because he used to believe blindly in the invincible and unavoidable solidarity of men which saved him from frustration and despair into which the preceding generation of novelists fell.

Conrad tells how the artist works. In his opinion, a good artist should completely blend the form with the substance and that it is the substance which should lend the form of piece of composition. This form, according to Conrad, should be able to make an appeal to varied temperaments; and he believes that this aim can be achieved only by conveying impressions through the senses because, according to Conrad, temperament cannot be persuaded by any other method or with any other contrivance whether the temperament is collective or individual. All art, according to Conrad, is primarily an appeal to the sense, which can be achieved equally by painting, sculpture and music (which is also poetry). He says:

"It is only through complete, unswerving devotion to the perfect blending of form and substance, only through an unremitting never-discouraged care for the shape and ring of sentences that an approach can be made to plasticity, to colour and that the light of magic-suggestiveness may be brought to play for an evanescent instant over the commonplace surface of words; of the old, old words, worn thin, defaced by ages of careless usage."[4]

I have already said that Conrad's purpose or aim is to seek the truths of life, to help the readers in catching the rhythm, the music, the groans and lamentations of life or, in other words, to make the readers feel the pulse, the tension and the restlessness of life and on top of all, to present or prove the invincible bonds of friendship and solidarity which run through mankind in all ages. Let us see what Conrad says in this connection:

> "My task which I am trying to achieve is by the power of the written word to make you feel, it is, before all, to make you see. That and no more and it is everything. If I succeed, you shall find there; encouragement, consolation, fear, charm—all you demand—and perhaps, also that glimpse of truth for which you have forgotten to ask. To snatch in a moment of courage, from the remorseless rush of time, passing phase of life, is only the beginning of the task. The task approached rescued fragment before all eyes in the light of sincere mood. It is to show its vibrations, passion within the core of each convincing moment. In a single minded attempt of kind, if one be deserving and fortunate, one may perchance attain to such clearness of sincerity that at last the presented vision of regret, of pity or terror or mirth shall awaken in the heart of beholders, that feeling of unavoidable solidarity; of the solidarity in the mysterious origin, in toil, in joy, in hope, in uncertain fate which binds men to each other and all mankind to the visible world."[5]

Conrad believes that man lives in society and that there is a sense of community in him, that man is linked up with other men by a common bond of solidarity; and it is the job of the artist to awaken in man the feeling of solidarity which may be temporarily concealed or suppressed by the various selfish desires of man. He further believes that it is through the fleeting moments of mental and bodily existence that man achieves the aim of his life and the artist too achieves the aim or purpose or mission of his art. Conrad further tells that in order to achieve such aim, the artist has to give up rule for that although he has to take the help of all the rules and all the formulas so far followed or applied by the various artists in the same field. It is worthwhile to see what he says in this connection warning all against the pitfalls into which an artist may get involved:

> "It is evident that he, who rightly or wrongly, holds by the convictions expressed above, cannot be faithful to any of the temporary formulas of his craft. The enduring part of them—the truth which each only imperfectly veils—should abide with him as the most precious of his possessions, but they all: Realism, Romanticism, Naturalism, even the unofficial

> Sentimentalism is exceedingly difficult to get rid of all these gods, must, after a short period of fellowship, abandon him, even on the very threshold of the temple, to the stammering of his conscience and to the outspoken consciousness of the difficulties of his work."[6]

He further explains his theory of art:

> "Sometimes, stretched at ease in the shade of a roadside tree, we watch the motions of a labourer in a distant field and after a time begin to wonder languidly as to what the fellow be at. We watch the movement of his body, the waving of his arms, we see him bend down, stand up and hesitate again. It may add to the charm of an idle hour to be told the purpose of his exertions. If we know, he is trying to lift a stone to dig a ditch, to uproot a stump, we look with a more real interest at his efforts: we are disposed to condone the jar of his agitation up the restfulness of the landscape; and even if in a brotherly frame of mind, we may bring ourselves to forgive his failure. We understood his object and after all the fellow has tried, and perhaps he had not the strength, and perhaps he had not the knowledge. We forgive to go our way and forget. And so it is the workman of art. Art is long and life is short and success is very far off. And thus doubtful of strength to travel so far, we talk a little about the aim of art which like life itself, is inspiring, difficult, obscured by mists. It is not the clear logic of a triumphant conclusion; it is not in the unveiling of one of those heartless secrets which are called the Laws of Nature. It is not less great, but only more difficult."[7]

I feel that in Conrad's theory of art, life has form and colour; life has sunshine and shadows. It has moments of glory and moments of despair. Most of our approaches and visions are partial; most of them are coloured and prejudiced. Indeed, it is very difficult to have an integral vision, to have an approach which is all circumscribing, all absorbing. But a real artist strives to attain such a position. The real artist is not an entertainer, though he appeals to our feeling of delight and wonder. He is not an escapist and his feet are firmly transplanted in the mother earth. He is not a formalist; he seeks to harmonize the claims of form and content in his work. Now let us see the concluding remarks of Conrad regarding a real artist:

> "To arrest for the space of a breath, the hands busy about the work of the earth and compel men entranced by the sight of distant goals to glance for a moment at the surrounding vision of form and colour, of sunshine and shadows, to make them pause for a look, for a sigh, for a smile, such is the aim, difficult and evanescent and reserved only for a very few to achieve. But sometimes, by the deserving and the fortunate, and even that task is

> accomplished—behold! All the truths of life is there: a moment of vision, a sigh, a smile and the return to an eternal rest."[8]

Conrad is undoubtedly a great realist and also a great romantic. He believes in facts as well as imagination, each of which should play upon the other in order to produce a good piece of art. In most of his works, Conrad has drawn, used and reflected the experiences of his own life. Conrad does not believe in the impersonal order of art which has been championed by the naturalists. In Conrad's opinion, the novels or stories of these naturalists are examples of the worst vices of the old convention of arbitrary omniscience in fiction. The novelist says that there should be a real presentation of life, of life is no literary: his novels or stories used his vast experiences of life, particularly of sea life which have entered the very web and woof of Conrad's works of art. He studied the ocean, the sea-men in their moments of glory as well as of weakness and has depicted in his novels with the colour of his imagination all such experiences, all such moments of heroism and adventure. Conrad has his own view points about his sea-life, sea experiences, seamen and the great world of water. Sea life had been Conrad's life. It had been his own self-sufficient and self satisfying possession. Then the change came over the spirit of his dream. His past had, by the force of his work, become one of the sources of what he might call, for want of better word, his inspiration—of the inner force which sets the pen in motion.

But Conrad is not a writer of mere sea tales; his novels and stories are not merely stories of travels and exploration or adventure. His are the stories of human life. His is the whole world where we find men like Captain Anthony, Singleton and Whalley—honest, faithful and disciplined—having the cardinal virtues of a sailor, like Jim and Razumov—honest but uncertain, faithful but timid at the final moment-taking shelter in the fortress of their own weakness—and like Williams and Kurtz—rogues, exploiters and marauders. With the sea life as the background, Conrad presents to us the real world that we are in.

From his sea-experience he has come to know of several cardinal virtues of life. They are loyalty, discipline, self-devotion and sense of human solidarity. These are needed if one has to fight against the ferocity of nature. These are required if one has to face the challenges of life. So Conrad colours his sea-experiences with his imagination, with his attitude towards life. He observes everything minutely. Facts are there, but the reactions are his own. And he records his reaction—reactions born of his peculiar mental make-up and innate disposition. Fiction to him is human history. In the case of Conrad it stands on firmer ground, being based on the reality of forms and the observation of social phenomena whereas history is based on documents—on second hand impression. This human history is often the history of Conrad himself. We find in him a sense of moral isolation but he is fully alive to his responsibilities and duties. He is aware of the hostile world whose mysteries he wants to explore. He is always conscious of his conscience and very sardonically speaks out a truth through Razumov of 'Under Western Eyes'—"All a man can betray is his conscience."[9]

He seeks to bring out this moral and spiritual crisis in his characters through various methods—impressionistic, psychological and narrative. He and his characters are engaged in self-discovery. But can the man in isolation get peace of mind and enjoy freedom? Can he ignore the society and outer world? And can he be really lovely? Conrad says that a man can run away from everything, from everywhere, but he cannot run away from his conscience. It follows a man like the hounds of heaven. He may ignore it and seek to forget it by indulging in nefarious activities, by drowning himself in sexual and other perversities. Still he cannot get freedom, because 'freedom of one is conditioned by the freedom of the other', says Morton Danwen Zabel:

> "The man who is alone in the world can never escape, for he is always with himself. Unless he is morally abandoned beyond the point of significance through profligacy or irresponsibility, he lives in the company of a ruthless inquisitor, a watcher who never sleeps, a perpetually vigilant judge, with his instinct of identity, the moral imperative of existence."[10]

M.D. Zabel further says about Joseph Conrad in the same breath:

> "The romantic element in the work of Joseph Conrad, like the romantic impulse in his nature, was never effaced. It persisted as basis of his popularity of the excesses of style and treatment of the sea, of women and of fortune as inscrutable entities, in his exotic and the miraculous in human fate and character, in the fatigued naiveté of fatalism that reasserts itself in his last three novels. But if it was not effaced, it was recognized. Conrad himself admitted an inherent romanticism as a component of his imagination and of his ordeal in moral and creative responsibilities. He referred to it late in life in a passage of apology. The romantic feeling of reality was in me as inborn faculty. This in itself may be a curse, but when disciplined by a sense of personal responsibility and recognition of the hard facts of existence shared

> with the rest of mankind becomes a point of view from which the very shadows of life appear endowed with an internal glow. And such romanticism is not a sin. It is none the worse for the knowledge of truth. It only tried to make the best of it, hard as it may be, and in this hardness discovers a certain aspect of beauty. His success came when responsibility and discipline opposed the self indulgence which a romantic impulse had encouraged in his early emotions and sensibility. When these correctiveness assert themselves in its pages, they produce the rigour of style and feeling which stiffens and gives structure to the natural extravagance of his emotions, his impulsiveness in sentiment, the untested enthusiasm of his responses to scene, character and experience. Conrad's development as an artist—with due allowance made for the weakening powers of his later novels—reproduces the ordeal of self-mastery and moral exoneration which he repeatedly dramatised in the lives of his characteristic heroes.

The measure of Conrad's character and his artistry may be taken from the fact that neither his sense of honour nor his sense of realism permitted him to betray the conscience which it took him half his life to discover in himself and the other half to test and dramatise in his books."[11]

Joseph Conrad is a tireless experimenter for whom the novel is a plastic form to be reshaped in accordance with his changing intention and design. H.G. Wells placed Conrad in the same category of novelists as Henry James and when Wells spoke of their immense artistic preoccupations, he was quite right. All his life, Conrad remained busy with these artistic preoccupations and went on experimenting with the technique of the novel. Writing on Henry James he said in 1905:

> "All creative art is magic, is evocation of the unseen in forms—persuasive, enlightening, familiar and surprising, for the edification of mankind, pinned down by the conditions of its existence to the earnest consideration of the most insignificant tides of reality."

Action in its essence, the creative art of a writer of fiction, may be compared to rescue work carried out against cross gusts of wind, swaying the action of a great multitude. It is rescue-work, this snatching of vanishing phases of turbulence, disguised in fair words, out of the native obscurity into a light, where the struggling forms may be seen, seized upon, endowed with the only possible form of permanence in this world of relative values—the permanence of memory. And the multitude feels it obscurely too; since the demand of the individual to the artist is, in effect, the cry. "Take me out of myself," meaning really out of my perishable activity into the light of consciousness. But everything is relative and the light of consciousness is only enduring, merely the most enduring of the things of the earth, imperishable only as against the short-lived work of our industrious hands.

When the last aqueduct shall have crumbled to pieces, the last airship fallen to the ground, the last blade of grass have died upon dying earth, man, indomitable by his training in resistance to misery and pain shall set this undiminished light of his eyes against feeble glow of the sun. The artistic faculty, of which each of us has a minute grain, may find its voice in some individual of that last group, gifted with a power of expression and courageous enough to interpret the ultimate experience of mankind in terms of his temperament, in terms of art. I do not mean to say that he would attempt to beguile the last moments of humanity by an ingenious tale. It would be too much to expect from humanity. I doubt the heroism of the hearers. As to the heroism of the artist, no doubt, is necessary, there would be on his part no heroism. The artist in his calling of interpreter creates because he must."[12]

In the preface to 'The Nigger of Narcissus' Conrad describes his own artistic endeavours. Really Conrad was conscious of the same artistic problems that confronted Henry James. It was the fundamental problems of rendering in a suitable form in fiction, the myriad forms of human consciousness. The word consciousness itself is used by Conrad, and the evocation of the unseen in forms persuasive, becomes the sole object of his novelistic technique. Conrad remained to the last day of his life a conscious and deliberate artist. Like Henry James, he was constantly calculating the effect of his art.

The job of the novelist, as Conrad realised it, is to render life accurately and realistically, according to his own vision of life. Conrad lays it down as a simple principle, at least for himself as a novelist, that a novelist must exclude all comments about the characters in his story and must suppress consciously all personal prejudices.

Prejudices spring essentially from thought and have very little to do with an artist's awareness and apprehension of life. Prejudices are not a part of an artist's vision and as such are not to be permitted to mould an artist's outlook. He suggests that an artist is basically a person who sees and not a person who reasons. Conrad was quite explicit in this matter when he declared "Fiction—if it, at all aspires to be art, appeals to temperament and that such an appeal to be effective, must be an impression conveyed through the senses." (Preface— 'The Nigger of the Narcissus').

Thus Conrad lays maximum stress on 'temperament' and its communication to others through an art-form, be it sculpture, painting, music or fiction. Mrs. Virginia Woolf spoke of this very thing over and over again and tried to prefect this particular art of communication of temperament in her novels and stories. Conrad also says the same thing.

Not that he was always successful, not that he succeeded every time he attempted but on the whole he did succeed in this difficult task:

> "He succeeded, one might say, in spite of himself, for these were times when he too called in persuasion, when, for one reason or another, perhaps because his self-annihilation, the abandonment of personality in the conception, was not perfectly complete. He appeals at times, he must appeal again and again, to the intellect to ratify the vision."[13]

Thus social and material problems were not his subjects nor was he interested in sex or marriages. His main aim was the mind and soul of characters. His themes are mainly two. He chose to make his own experiences of sea-life and tropical areas as the subject matter of his novels. Secondly, he desired to use the novel to illustrate one fundamental fact of life—fidelity and faith between man and man, while leading with this moral problem of evil in human life and its consequences. We find an impressionist document in the preface to 'The Nigger of Narcissus' but much of Conrad's critical position there is also consonant with that of the symbolists. Joseph Conrad also wrote in a letter that in 'The Nigger of Narcissus' he had tried 'to get through the veil of details at the essence of life.'[14]

And this avowal of transcendental perspective later recurs even more explicitly:

> "How fine it could..." Conrad wrote to Ford, "if the idea had a substance and words a magic power, if the invisible could be snared into a shape."[15]

Conrad expressed this wish to make the idea visible a month before he began "Heart of Darkness", a work which, among other things, is generally reckoned with the supreme example of Conrad's importance in the modern symbolist literary tradition. Marvin Mudrick, for example, declares with almost pardonable hyperbole that after 'Heart of Darkness', the recorded moment the word was irrecoverably symbol.[16] 'Heart of Darkness' is taken as a major example of the symbolist novel in William York Tindall's 'The Literary Symbol'.[17]

The base of the analysis of Mudrick is based on the way Conrad developed the moral resources inherent in every recorded sensation. In this way he implies that in 'Heart of Darkness' Conrad gave a larger symbolic meaning to an impressionist recording of particular experience. This novel is the key work for examining the relation of symbolist and impressionist elements in Joseph Conrad for another reason, According to Ian Watt interpretation of its symbolism continues to provoke much critical controversy.

Conrad's metaphor clearly implies the complementary, even the symbolic, relationship of the impressionist and the symbolist aspects of the narrative as a whole. The symbolist aspect mainly depends on the geometric nature of the haze, the outer sphere of larger meaning. It is intangible and theoretically infinite, since like St. Augustine's God and unlike the husk of a nut, it lacks any ascertainable circumference; and yet it depends on the finite glow. Thus the combination of Marlow's two spheres constitutes a symbol precisely in Carlyle's sense of it—"the Infinite is made to blend itself with Finite, to stand visible, and as it were, attainable there."[19]

The impressionist component of the passage is mainly evident in the sensory qualities of Conrad's two spheres. The narrative depicts a meaning which is only a fitfully and tenuously visible as a hitherto unnoticed presence of dust particles and water vapour in what normally looks like a dark void. In this there is a clear parallel with one of the new features of impressionist painting. Cloud Monet, for example, told about the critics who mocked his obscurity:

> "Poor blind idiots. They want us to see everything clearly, even through the fog."[20]

The difficulty of seeing is not a gratuitous defense of the public; haze in Monet and even more explicitly in Conrad's image—is not an accidental atmospheric interference which stands between us and the 'real object'; the difficulty and the obscurity are essential parts to what the artist is trying to convey.

Much the same idea, and expressed in a similar metaphor, occurs in a classic later statement on the novel in 'Modern Fiction' by Virginia Woolf.[21] In this Mrs. Woolf exempts Conrad's together with Hardy, from her charge against the "ill fitting vestments" of the traditional novel, and of the Edwardians, H.G. Wells, Arnold Bennett John Galsworthy."[22] The basic objection of Mrs. Virginia Woolf is that if we 'look within' ourselves, we find, "a myriad impressions quite unrelated to anything that goes on in the traditional novel; and if we could express 'this unknown and uncircumcised spirit' of life freely, there would be no plot, no comedy, no tragedy, no love interest or catastrophe in the accepted style and perhaps not a single button sewn on as the Bond Street tailors would have it."[23]

For Mrs. Woolf finally affirms:

> "Life is not a series of gig-lamps symmetrically arranged; life is a luminous halo, a semi-transparent envelope surrounding us from the beginning of consciousness to the end."[24]

The basic metaphor of Virginia Woolf, 'the luminous halo', is impressionist in nature, but it is used to describe an aim for the novel very like the characteristic symbolist attempt to reach outwards, to penetrate the semi-transparent, and therefore semi-opaque, envelope of the world outside. With the impressionist painters, the first object of creation is light; and with the symbolists it is most characteristically an inner light of the spirit which illuminates a part of the surrounding darkness.[25]

Now let us have a look what Ian Watt wants to say:

> "Before applying the description of Marlow's mode of story-telling to a passage from "Heart of Darkness", a brief historical perspective seems necessary; for, both in their origins and in their later course through modern literature, impressionism and symbolism are essentially manifestations of various general tendencies which first came to prominence in the romantic period; both are anti traditional assertions of the private individual vision; and they took their full shape during the epistemological crisis of the late nineteenth century, a crisis most familiar to literary history under the twin rubrics of the death of God and the disappearance of the omniscient author."[26]

"Impressionism" as a specifically aesthetic term was apparently launched in 1874 by a journalist Louis Leroy—to ridicule the affronting formlessness of the pictures exhibited at the Salon des Independents, and particularly of Claude Monet's painting entitled "Impression: Sunrise."

"In one way or another all the main Impressionism from Monet to Renoir, made it their aim to render the appearance of objects as they saw them under particular atmospheric conditions an aim which as E.H. Gombrich has shown," allots the impressionists a decisive role in the process of art's long transition from portraying what all men know to portraying what the individual actually sees."[27]

This transition is recorded in the history of the word "Impressions" and its cognets, a history which embodies in more general terms the growing distinction between the public systems of knowledge—what all men know—and the ephemeral indefiniteness of private experience what the individual actually sees. The concentration of philosophical thought upon epistemological problems from Descartes and Hume onwards made the relation between individual sensation and ascertainable truth increasingly problematic; and the distinction found more radical expression at the end of the eighteenth century, when the increasingly pervasive authority of a mechanistic and sensational psychology in effect drove the religious, imaginative, emotional and aesthetic orders of being into the private and internal world of the individual. After the romantics this process took a more deeply skeptical direction, which was most memorably expressed in the famous conclusion to 'The Renaissance' (1868-73), where Peter speaks of how 'each mind keeping as a solitary prisoner its own dream of a world' can actually experience directly only 'the passage and dissolution of impressions, images sensations.

The critical thought of Peter, and of the nineties, are both embodiments of a fusion between various Impressionist and symbolist were exactly contemporary; Verlaine, Rimband and Mallarme wrote during the hey day of the impressionist painters in the seventies, although symbolism as a conscious movement came a little later-in poetry when Jean Moreas wrote his manifesto in 1886, and in painting at the Cafe Volpin's exhibition in 1889. Compared to the views of earlier painters and writers, there were many parallels between the attitudes of the adherents of symbolism and impressionism, both in painting and poetry; they fully agreed in rejecting intellectual conceptualization and established artistic traditions in the name of expressing a directly-apprehended personal and subjective vision.

It is true in one important respect that the impressionists and symbolists took logically opposite direction. The impressionist painters began with the outside world as it appeared to their own subjective perception where as the symbolist painters wished, as Morean put it:

> "to clothe the idea in perceptible form; in effect the two schools differed in approaching their task from different ends of the same newly-intensified polarity between individual consciousness and external reality."[28]

In literature the symbolists and especially Mallarme and later Valery while just as opposed to logical conceptualization as any impressionist, nevertheless, wanted to get larger ideas into literature; somehow, although they were ideas of a very special kind; ideas which belonged only to the inner world of the consciousness, which only could be summoned through the portals of the creative imagination, and which were only manifested to the senses of the artist or his audience in the shape of symbols.

Here symbolism must be seen as part of the same historical process which produced the individualist and the subjective direction of impressionism, since the imagination and the symbol are distinctively romantic and post-romantic preoccupations. The process by which the individual mind attributed a larger intellectual or emotional meaning to particular objects and events was hardly a problem in earlier periods, because the whole universe was generally assumed to, constitute a fixed order in which every item had its communally-agreed meaning—most obviously in mythology which gave a spiritual role to everything in the external world. Men could hardly be consciously concerned with symbolism when the larger meaning of objects was hardly established, as with the cross, for instance, or the apple. But the Romantic writers felt impelled to assign their own personal symbolic meanings to natural objects, to mountains, birds and flowers; and they did so by creating new orders of meaning which were not those of the established orthodoxies but of the individual imagination. After Blake and Wordsworth it was commonly assumed that the poet had access to previously unknown imminent connections between the external world and spiritual reality.

This general epistemological assumption is reflected in one of the characteristic expressive idioms of modern literature. The post-romantic symbol is likely to be private rather than public; but it is not intended to stand for a single and definable concept. Even the poets who were most attached to satiric or transcendental beliefs tend in their writing to rely primarily on the many natural connotations of their images; Shelley's 'Skylark', Keats' 'Nightingale' or 'The swans of Mallarme' of Yeats–none of these are univocal or allegorical symbols; their meanings arise from the varied inherent suggestions of the poetic object and only to the extent that these are mobilized in the poem so that the reader concretely experiences all the implications of seeing and not sceing, singing and not singing, soaring and not soaring. The essential meaning of these symbolic images is established in a way quite unlike those traditional in allegory, a way that bears out Yeats' contrast between a symbol, which was, "the only possible expression of some individual essence, a transparent lamp about a spiritual flame," and allegory, which was "one of many possible representations of an embodied thing or familiar principle that belong (ed) to fancy and not imagination."[29]

Yeats' metaphor of the lamp and the flame for the inherent, natural and personal way that object and meaning come together in modern symbolism and impressionism, is fairly close to Conrad's metaphor of the two spheres; and both of them implicitly require a special kind of symbolic interpretation from the critic.

The symbolic images described by Yeats can only carry multiple suggestions to the extent that they evoke all the potencies of particular individual experience; and the symbolist's method, therefore, makes much the same primary demand as 'impressionism or imagism'.[30] It is in inquiring the writer to render the object with an idiosyncratic immediacy of vision which is freed from any intellectual prejudgment or explanatory gloss. The reader must also feel that he is in the presence of an unfamiliar hierarchy of attention, it is, for instance, the emphasis of some details and the absence of others which makes it clear that the birds in the poems of Mallarme of Yeats are presented not for their ornithological or autobiographical interest, but for some other purpose, some larger complex of connecting values and meanings. These values and meanings are not stated but only the hypothesis of their hidden presence, it seems, could explain the special emphasis with which the writer's perceptions are conveyed; the obtrusive disparity between a particular image and the significance apparently attributed to it creates a semantic gap which we feel called on to fill with our own symbolic interpretation.

One logical result of this semantic gap and more generally of the characteristic idiom and objectives of impressionism and symbolism, has been to give a much more important, but also a much more difficult role to the literary critic. He is faced with task of explaining to the public, in discursive expository prose, a literature whose authors deliberately kept their works as free as possible from rational or conceptual definition. He confronts an incompleteness of utterance, an indeterminacy of meaning, a seemingly unconscious or random association of images, which simultaneously demand and defy logical exigencies. In the fiction which belongs primarily to the impressionist school, such as that of Stephen Crane, or to its imagist and later heritages, such as that of Hemingway, the idiosyncratic sequence of vivid particularities asks to be construed and translated into the realm of public discourse; but once translated into that expository language not much is left, and its residue of general meaning is likely, in the critics' rendition of it, to seem both meagre and ambiguous. The difficulty is even greater for writing with a strong symbolist element, where there is, in addition, a semantic gap to be bridged, and an intangible unifying essence to be discovered. In either case the critic is asked to provide a commentary which will transcend the epistemological problems which dominate the expressive idiom of the literature he is analyzing. No one wonder, then, that the modern critic is prone to an excessive metaphysical abstraction in aims and language, and to a notorious compulsion for extravagant symbol-hunting.

This last tendency, which was particularly powerful during the apogee of the prestige of literary criticism in the fifties, seems to have been partly based on the idea that the essence of symbolism lay, not in its attempt to suggest the larger possibilities of meaning behind individual experience, but in its use of an essentially esoteric purpose and method.

To conclude, the Conradion sentence is often full of abstract moralizing modifiers, and may try to alter our common associations, of 'Freedom and Servitude for example, Norman Sherry writes:

> "For freedom is ignoble and servitude is honourably austere: The independent of spring of the ignoble freedom of the slums full of disdain and hate for the austere servitude of the sea."[31]

This is unmistakably a Conradian voice; and again unmistakably what Mrs. Virginia Woolf would have characterised as masculine one: assured, overbearing, powerful, altering unanswerable truths, over-riding delicate nuance and exception. It is at its most confident where strong political convictions are at stake, so confident that commas and other punctuated pauses seem out of the question. The rhythm sweeps on and over-rides; commas and other punctuated pauses are instruments of hesitation and doubt.[32]

Here is a cablegram sent by Conrad in 1920, without a single "stop" in it. This commanding voice did not want to stop:

> "For Poles the sense of duty and the imperishable feeling of nationality preserved in the hearts and defended by the hands of their immediate ancestors to open struggles against the might of three powers and in indomitable defiance of crushing opposition for more than a hundred years is sufficient inducement to assist in reconstructing the independent dignity and usefulness of the reborn republic."[33]

And here is a letter written in 1899 on the subject of Boar War, which employs a Conradion variety of sentence structure and length:

"It is always unwise to begin a war which, to be effective, must be a war of extermination; it is positively imbecile to start it without a clear notion of what it means and to force on questions for immediate solution which are eminently fit to be left to time. There is an appalling fatuity in this business. If I am to believe Kipling this is a war undertaken for the cause of democracy".[34]

This angry rhetoric, passionate yet composed, complex in syntax-employing both the Conradian periodic sentence and a rolling rhythm is understandably provoked by his feelings about Russia and Russians, as the 1926 Author's 'Note to Under Western Eyes' suggests:

> "The ferocity and imbecility of an autocratic rule rejecting all legality and in fact basing itself upon complete moral anarchism provokes the no less imbecile and atrocious answer of a purely Utopian revolutionism encompassing destruction by the first means to hand, in the strange conviction that a fundamental change of hearts must follow the downfall of any given human institutions".[35]

Prof. Norman Sherry, one of the best critics of Joseph Conrad presents Conradian voice in this way which according to me is authentic:

> "This political assurance was accompanied by an unusual awareness of moral complexities, the certitude often masked deep doubts; the austere ethic could be undermined by sympathy for the outlaw. I argued in "Conrad the Novelist" that the larger structures of Conradian impressionism responded to temperamental needs. The novelist was aloof, evasive, distrustful of others and distrustful of himself, poetic and moralizing, be-mused by ambiguity. It was very important to his temperament that he should be able to penetrate it deeply yet suddenly and safely withdraw, and move from the concrete particular to the very large protective generalization. Hence the attraction of narrators interposed between the writer and the action; hence the chronological dislocations and sudden time shifts; hence the shifting visual perspective and the elaborate drama of conflicting witnesses bringing forward evidence that remains in doubt. We can love the intricacy of Conradian impressionism for its own sake; or for its power to control the reader's sympathy and judgment, and for its effectiveness in achieving the fullest meanings. But we should also recognize that it catered to the writers' psychological needs; to the demands of his imagination and his temperament. It helped the richest tonalities of the Conradian voice."[36]

Every great writer surprises in one way or another, and Conrad's' voice conveys more than its share of unexpected felicities. And greatness is hardly conceivable without the turbulence which is controlled by language or the imaginative flights which are subdued by syntax. But the final characteristic of the Conradian voice is "control." This temperamental control of its material is through lovely running rhythms and through the shifts from long sentences to short and short to long. The control is exerted by contemplative language. In spite of some fumbling early on and again towards the end of Conrad's writing career that voice can be heard almost from the beginning and right through the very end. The first true emergence of the Conradian voice can be found in "The Rescue", as Conrad suddenly takes a distant view of a glamorous past. Conrad began work on 'The Rescue' in 1896. 'The Rescue' was published in 1920, twenty four years after it was begun:

> "Did you follow with your ghostly eyes the quest of this obscure adventurer of yesterday you shade of forgotten adventures who in leather jerkins and sweating under steel helmets attacked with long rapiers the palisades of the strange heathen or musket on shoulder and match in cock guarded lonely forts built upon the banks of rivers that command good trade?".[37]

This voice is heard, through much quieter, in the unfinished "Suspense." Conrad visited Corsica for research on "Suspense" in 1921.

"His voice was unexpected when I heard it as your own signore. The evening shadows had closed about me just after I had seen to the west, on the edge of the world as it were, a lion miss his spring on a bounding deer. They went right away into the glow and vanished. It was as though I had dreamed."[38]

Cleanth Brooks says: "The novelist was not to tell the reader about what happened but to render it as action. Moreover, the action was not to be rendered with photographic fidelity but as it would make its impression upon a human observer".[39]

Hence Ford Madox Ford's name is found for the new art, 'Impressionism'. As Ford put it:

> "Conrad found salvation not in any machised form, but in the sheer attempt to produce in words life as it presents itself to the intelligent observer."[40]

Henry James is actually referring in this passage to a power of the novelist, but it is a power, which in some measure, any writer using a dramatic method must also demand of his reader. Conrad himself put it (in his "Preface to The Nigger of the Narcissus): "before all, to make you see"

In this way there is no doubt in it that "he is one of the great creative geniuses, but his personality is of the first order, he has through a sheer miracle, wrought ill-assorted elements into a strong synthesis. He has, in a learnt language, fashioned an irresistible style, loaded with the nervous impact, stern realities carried onward by a rhythm which not only multiplies their hard rigour but bathes it in a meditative music through which the soul catches an undertone of softer harmonies".[41]

I have tried to find in my own way, the first true emergence of the Conradian voice through the new literary cosmopolitanism of the twentieth century. It is Conrad who has broken the tight link which binds the artistic handling of a given tongue to the exclusive possession of an intellectual nationality.

References

1. Conrad, Joseph, "The Nigger of the Narcissus", Preface p. 5.
2. Conrad, Joseph, "The Nigger of the Narcissus", Preface p. 5.
3. Conrad, Joseph, "The Nigger of the Narcissus". (Surjeet publication), p. 5-6.
4. Conrad, Joseph, *Ibid.*, p. 7.
5. Conrad, Joseph, "The Nigger of the Narcissus". Edited with an Introduction and notes by Cedric Watts, Penguin Books, 1963.
6. *Ibid.*, p. 8.
7. *Ibid.*, p. 8-9.
8. *Ibid.*, p. 9.
10. Zabel Morton Dawen, "Craft and characters in Modern Fiction" New York, 1947, p. 91.
11. *Ibid.*, p. 92.
12. Conrad, Joseph, "Life and Letters". p. 14-15.
13. Conrad, Joseph, "A Personal Remembrance". Orient Longman; pp. 182-183.
14. 'A Letter of Conrad', (27th January, 1897).
15. 'Life and Letters', 2 Vols. (London, 1927).
16. Joseph Conrad ed. By Jacolyn Baines, 'A Critical Biography', (London, 1960), p. 223.
17. The originality of Conrad, Hudson Review, II (1958), p. 545-53.
18. The Literary Symbol, (New York, 1955), p. 86-91.
19. Conrad, Joseph, "Heart of Darkness" (Surjeet Publications), 1989, pp. 4-8.
20. Lecture of Lan Watt at the International Conference on Conrad at Canterbury (18 July, 1974).
21. Jean Renoir, 'My Father', translated by Randolph & Dorothy Weaver (Boston and Toronto, 1958), p. 174.
22. Modern Essay by Virginia Woolf, (1919).

23. "The Common Reader", London (1938), pp. 145-59.
24. *Ibid.,* p. 160.
25. Watt, lan, 'Impressionism & Symbolism' (18th July, 1974). International Conference at Contarbury, at Contarbury.
26. Watt, lan, 'Essay read at the 1974 meeting of the International Association of University Professors of English at Los Angeles (August 20).
27. E. H. Gombrich: The story of Art, 12th ed., p. 406.
28. Albert Skira & Jean Leymarie-'Impressionism', 2 Vols., pp. 123-24.
29. Ed. By Frank Kermode, 'The Romantic Image' (London, 1957), pp. 112-13.
30. Herbert N. Schniedan 'The Image & The Real', pp. 34-35.
31. Sherry, Norman, Prof. of English Literature, University of Lancaster, 'The Conradian Voice', p. 3, The Macmillan Press, 1979.
32. *Ibid.*
33. Conrad, Joseph, Life and Letters; p. 81.
34. *Ibid.,* p. 83.
35. Conrad, Joseph, 'Under Western Eyes', Surjeet Publication, p. 11.
36. Conrad, Joseph, 'A Commemoration', International conference on Conrad 1947, Ed, by Prof. Norman Sherry, Printed in G.B., London, Reprinted 1979.
37. Conrad, Joseph, 'The Rescue' Surjeet Publication Delhi, First Indian Reprint 1989, p. 35.
38. Conrad, Joseph, "Suspense" From "Serial to Book" Research Studies of the State College of Washington; Vol. III, No. 4, p. 310.
39. Brooks, Cleanth, 'Literary Criticism: A short history of Oxford', I, B. H. Publications, New Delhi, This is a Berzoi Book Published in 1847.
40. 'The Art of Fiction', in partial portraits (London and New York 1888). Reprinted in The Art of Fiction and other essays by Henry James, ed. Morris, Robert. (New York, 1948) p. 11.
41. *Ibid.,* p. 1334.

Bibliography

A. Primary Sources

1. Works of Joseph Conrad

'A SET OF SIX' (1908). Short Stories. Contains: 'Gaspar Ruiz', 'The Informer', 'The Brute', 'An Anarchist', 'The Duel', 'Il Conde'.

'ALMAYER'S FOLLY'—A Story of an Eastern River (1895). Novel.

'AN OUTCAST OF THE ISLANDS' (1896). Novel.

'CHANCE—A Tale in Two Parts' (1914). Novel.

'LORD JIM—A Tale' (1990). Novel.

'NOSTROMO'—A Tale of the Seaboard (1904). Novel.

'NOTES ON LIFE AND LETTERS' (1921). Essays.

'ROMANCE—A novel' (1903). Novel. In collaboration with Ford Madox Hueffer.

'SOME REMINISCENCE' (1912). Novel. This title appears in the Collected Editions as a 'Personal Record'.

'TALES OF UNREST' (1898). Short Stories, Contains: ' Karain: a Memory' 'The Idiots', 'An Outpost of Progress', 'The Return', 'The Lagoon'.

'THE ARROW OF GOLD'—A Story between Two Notes (1919). Novel.

'THE INHERITORS'—An extravagant story (1901). Novel. In collaboration with Ford Madox Hueffer.

'THE MIRROR OF THE SEA'—Memories and Impressions (1906). Autobiography

'THE NIGGER OF THE NARCISSUS'—A Tale of the Sea (1897). Novel.

'THE RESCUE'—A Romance of the Shallows (1920). Novel.

'THE ROVER' (1924). Novel.

'THE SECRET AGENT'—A drama in Four Acts (1923). Drama.

'THE SECRET AGENT'—A Simple Tale (1907). Novel.

'THE SHADOW LINE—A Confession' (1917). Novel.

'TWIXT LAND AND SEA'—Tales (1912). Short Stories. Contains: 'A Smile of Fortune', 'The Secret Sharer', 'Freya of the Seven Isles'.

'TYPHOON', and Other Stories (1903). Short Stories. Contains: 'Typhoon', 'Amy Foster', 'Falk', 'Tomorrow'.
'UNDER WESTERN EYES' (1911). Novel.
'VICTORY—An Island Tale' (1915). Novel.
'WITHIN THE TIDES—Tales' (1915). Short Stories. Contains: 'The Planter of Malta', 'The Partner.' 'The Inn of the Two Witches', 'Because of the Dollars'.
'Youth—A Narrative' and Two Other Stories (1902). Short Stories. Contains: 'Youth', 'Heart of Darkness', 'The End of the Tether'.

2. Letters

Blackburn, William—Joseph Conrad: Letters to William Blackwood and David S. Meldrum. Durhan KC: Duke University press, 1958.
Conrad's Polish Background—Letters to and from polish friends, ED. Zdzislaw Najder tr. Halina Carrol, Oxford 1964.
Conrad to a friend, 150 Selected letters from Conrad to Richard Curle, ed, Richard Curle, Double Day, Doran, 1928.
Conrad Joseph—Letters to his Wife, London, Privately printed, 1927.
Conrad. Joseph—Letter to R.B. Cunninghame Graham, ed. C.T. watts, Cambridge, 1969.
Conrad-Galsworthy, A Record of their Friendship in Letters Midway Autumn, 1968.
Garnett, Esward—Letter from Joseph Conrad, 1895-1924 Indian Polis: Bobbs Merrill, 1988.
Gee, John A., and Sturn, Paul J.—Letters of Joseph Conrad to Marguerite Poradowska, 1890-1920 (New Haven, com. Yale University Press, 1940).
Garnett, Esward—Letters from Joseph Conrad, 1895 to 1924, London, 1928.
Joan, Aubry G—Joseph Conrad—Life and Letter 2 Vols. Double Day, Doran, 1927.
Letters from Conrad Joseph, 1895-1925, ed. Edward Garnett, Bobbs Merrill, 1928.
Letters from Conrad Joseph to Marguerite Poradowska—1890 to 1920, tr. And ed. John A. Gee and Paul J. Sturn, Yale, 1940.
Letters of Conrad Joseph to Willaim Blackwood and Davids S. Meldrum, ed. William Blackburn, Duke, 1958.
Marrmot, H.V.—The life and Letters of Joseph Conrad.
Najder, Zdzislaw—Joseph Conrad's Letters to Roger, P Casement., Polish perspectives No. 12, 1974.

B. Secondary Sources

1. Works on Joseph Conrad

Duebe, Maurice—Criticism of Joseph Conrad: A selected check list with an index to studies of separate works. Modern Fiction studies. Vol. 1. February 1955.
Conrad, Borys—My Father: Joseph Conrad, Calder & Bayers, London, 1970.

Conrad, Jessie—Joseph Conrad and his circle: Dutton. 1935.
Cox, C.B.—Joseph Conrad: The Modern imagination, Dent 1974.
Crankshaw, Edmard—Joseph Conrad: Some Aspects of the Art of the Novel, Macmillan, 2nd Edition. 1975.
Curle, Richard—Joseph Conrad: A Study, 1974.
Conrad, Jessie—Joseph Conrad as I knew him. 1926.
Curle. Richard—The last Twelve Years of Joseph Conrad, 1928.
Crever, Lawrence—Conrad's Short Ficrion, Berkley & Los Angeles, University of California Press. 1969.
Clemns, Cyrill—A chart with Joseph Conrad.
Coustillas, Pierre—Conrad and Gissing: A study in Joseph Conrad, Edited by Claude, Thomas, Montpellier, 1975.
Daniel, R. Schwarz—Novelists on Novel, The Macmillan press Ltd. 1982.
Dalexki, H. M—Joseph Conrad: The way of Dispossession, Holmes & Meier. New York 1976.
Ford, Ford Madox—Joseph Conrad: A Personal Remembrance, Little Brown, 1924.
Fleishmen, Airom—Conrad's Politics: Baltimore, 1967.
Forjeon, Eleanor—The Last Four years, 1958.
Guerard, Albert—Joseph Conrad: the Novelist, Harvard, 1958.
Gordon, John Dozier—Joseph Conrad: The Making of a Novelist.
Craver, Lawrence—Conrad's Short Fiction, University of California Press. 1968.
Galsworthy, John—Reminiscences of Conrad and Preface to Conrad's Plays in Castles in Spain. 1927.
G, Jean Aubry—Vie de Conrad, 1947.
Guerard, Albert—Joseph Conrad: the Novelist: Harvard University Press, 1958.
Guetti, James—'Heart of Darkness': The Failure of Imagination in his limits of Metaphor. Cornell University Press. 1967.
Hewitt, De.—Conrad: A Reassessment, 1952.
Hay, Kloise Knapp—The Political Novels of Joseph Conrad, The University of Chicago Press, 1963.
Harkness, Bruce—Conrad's 'The Secrat Sharer' and the Critics. Belmont Calif. Wadsworth 1962.
Haugh, Robert—Joseph Conrad's Discovery in Design; University of Oklaroma Press, 1957.
Ray, Eloise Knapp—The Political Novels of Joseph Conrad, University of Chicago Press 1963.
Hemitt, Douglas—Conrad: A Reassessment; Bones & Bones Cambridge 1952.
Howe, Irving—Conrad: Order and Anarchy in his politics and the Novel. New York Horizon Press and Meridien books 1957.
Higdon, D.L.—The Text and Context of Conrad's First Critical Essay, Edited by a Gillon and Krzyzanowski, New York, 1975.
Johnson, Bruce—Conrad's Models of Mind, Minnea Polis. University of Minnesota Press 1971.
Karl, Fredrick R.—A Reader's Guide to Joseph Conrad, Noonday Press, New York, 1960.

Kirschner, Paul—Conrad and Maupassant: Morai Solitude and A smile of Fortune—Review of English studies, Vol. 7, 1966.

Krzyzanowski, Ludwik—Joseph Conrad: Centennial Essays, New York, 1960.

Karl, Fredrick—A Reader's Guide to Joseph Conrad, New York, 1969.

Loft, Kenneth A., and Eugene P, Sheehy—Joseph Conrad at Mid Century, Editors and Studies, 1895-1955, University of Minnesota Press, 1957.

Mudrick, Marvin—Conrad: A Collection of critical Essays, Prentice Hall, 1967.

Meyer, Bernard, C.M.D.—Joseph Conrad: a Psychoanalytic Biography, Princeton, 1967,

Morf, Gustav—The Polish Heritage of Joseph Conrad, Sampson Low, Marston, 1930.

Mosor, Thomas—Joseph Conrad: Achievement and Decline, Harvard, 1957.

Megroz, R.L.—A Talk with Joseph Conrad, 1926.

Mencken, H.L.—Essay on Conrad in a book of Prefaces, 1917.

Mc Call, Dan—The Meaning in Darkness: A Response to a Psychoanalytical Study of Conrad, College English Vol. XXIX, 1968.

Mayer, Bernard C. M. D.—Joseph Conrad: A Psychoanalytical Biography, Princeton, N. J.—Princeton University Press, 1968.

Megroz, Rodolphe Lovis—Joseph Conrad: Mind and Method, London, 1931.

Mayer, Bernard C.—Joseph Conrad: A Psychoanalytical Biography, Princeton, 1967.

Morf, Gustov—The Polish Heritage of Joseph Conrad, London, 1930.

Moser, Thomas C.—Joseph Conrad: Achievement and Decline, Cambridge Mass, 1957.

Mursis, Ugo—The True "Discover" of Joseph Conrad's Literary Telent and other Notes on Conradian Biography, Vorse, 1971.

Palmer, John A.—Joseph Conrad's Fiction: A study in Literary Growth, Cornell, 1968.

Perry, John Oliver, 'Action Vision or Voice': The Moral Dilemmas in Conrad's Tale-Telling Modern Fiction Studies, Vol. X, 1964.

Passkowski, Lech—Conrad in Australian Porta, 1967.

Randall, Dale B.J.—Joseph Conrad and Warrington Dawson: The Record of a Friendship, Durham, 1969.

Ruth, M. Stauffer—Joseph Conrad:His Romantic Realism, 1922.

Roting, J.H.—Conrad and his Contemporaries, 1941.

Rosenfield, Clair—Paradise of Snakes: An Archetypal Analysis of Conrad's Political Novels, Chicago, University of Chicago Press, 1967.

Roussel Royal—The Metaphysics of Darkness: A Study in the Unity and Development of Conrad's (Fiction), Baltimore and London. The Johns Hopkins Press, 1971.

Rhys, Emest—An Interview with Joseph Conrad. The Bookman, 1922.

Sherry, Norman—Conrad's Eestern World, Cambridge, 1966.

Conrad's Western World, Cambridge, 1971.

Symons, Arthur—Notes on Joseph Conrad with Some unpublished letters, London, kyers, 1925.

Stauffer, Ruth M.—Joseph Conrad: His Romantic Realism, 1922.
Said Edward, W.—Joseph Conrad and the Fiction of Autobiography, Cambridge Mass Harvard University Press. 1966.
Schwarz, Daiel. R.—Conrad's 'Almayer's Folly' to 'Under Western Eyes', London Mecmillan Ithaca, N. Y. Cornnell university press 1930.
Secor, Robert—The Rhetoric of Shifting Perspective: Conrad's Victory, Pennsil—vania State University Studies no 32, University Park. 1971.
Stallman, Robert. W.—The art of Joseph Conrad: A Critical Symposium, East Lancing Mich. Michigan State University Press 1960.
Schawab, A.I.—Conrad's American Speeches and His Reading From Victory, Modern Philology, 1965.
Sherry, Norman.—Conrad: The Critical Heritage, London, 1973.
Sherry, Norman.—Joseph Conrad: A Commemoration, London, 1976.
Sutherland, J.G.—At sea with Joseph Conrad, Boston, 1922.
Teets Bruce and Gerber, Helmut.—Joseph Conrad: An Annointed Bibliography of Writing about Him, De kalb, 1971.
Walpole, Hugh—Joseph Conrad, 1916.
Woolf, Virginia—Essay on Conrad in the Common Reader, 1925.
Warner, Oliver—Joseph Conrad, 1951.
Wise, J.T.—A Bibliography of the writings of Joseph Conrad, 1921. A Conrad library Collected by T.J. Wise, London, 1928.
Warren, Robert Penn—Introduction to Nostromo, New York Modern Library, 1951.
Wiley, Paul L.—Conrad's Measure of Man: Madison University of Wiscons Press, Toronto Burns and Mac Eachern, 1954.
Wright, Walter F.—Romance and Tragedy in Joseph Conrad; Levicoln Nebr. University of Nebraska Press, 1949.
Zabel, Norton Douwen—Conrad in his Craft and Character in Modern Fiction; New York, Viking 1957.
Zeromaski, Stefan—Joseph Conrad Preface to J. Conrad.
Zuckerman, Jerome—A Smile of Fortune Conrad's Interesting.
Zeromaski, Stefan—Joseph Conrad edited by Stanislaw Pigon, Warsaw, 1963.

2. General Criticism on Fiction and Literature

Aubrey, G. Jean—The sea Dreamer, 1957.
Allot, Miriam—Novelists on the Novel;Routledge & Kegan paul, London, 1959.
Auerbach, Erich—Nimesis. The Representation of Reality in Western Literature, Will and Trask Princeton University press, 1953.
Askenazy, Szymon—Vwayi (Remarks) Geneva, 1916.
Baines, Jocelyn—Joseph Conrad: A Critical biography, (New York Mc. Graw Hill, 1960).
Beach, Joseph Warren—Impressionism in Conrad—The 20th Century Novel Studies in Technique, New York, Appleton Century, 1932.

Blackmur, R.P.—Eleven Essays in the European Novel (New York, Carbinger Books, 1954).
Booth, Waynec—The Rhetoric of Fiction, (Chicago, University of Chicago press, 1961).
Burke, Kenneth—The Philosophy of Literary Form, Rev. Bdn. (New York. Vintage Books, 1957).
Blackmore, E.—The British Mercantile Marine—A short Historical Review, London, 1887.
Collins Co build Dictionary of the English language, Collins London and Glasgow, Richard Clay Ltd. Bungay, Suffolk.
Cassirer, Ernst—The Logic of the Humanities, Trans. Clarence Smith Howe (New Haven Conn: yale University press 1961).
Crew, Frederic—The Power of Darkness; partisan Review, Vol. XXXIV, Autumn 1967.
Conrad, Wells and the two voices proceeding of the Modern Language Association, October, 1973.
Daumer, Morton Zabel—Craft and Character in Modern Fiction; The Viking press Icn.
Dangerfield, George—The Strong Death of Liberal England, 1010-1914, New York: Capricorn 1961.
Douglas, Norman—Looking Book, London, 1931.
Eliot, T.S.—Selected Prose; Faber and Faber Hunt Bernard & Co. Ltd. Aylesbury.
Mike, Donald—The Tempest of Axel Heyst. Nineteenth Century Fiction, Vol. XVIII, September 1962.

Journals and Books

Bartlett, Arnold—Journals, Edited by New Man Flower Vols. I & 2, London, 1932.
Bojaraski Edmund A.—Conrad at the Cross Roads From Navigator to Novelist with New Biographical Mysteries, The Texas Quarterly Writer, 1968.
Bojaraski, E.A., and Stevens, K.R.—Joseph Conrad and the Falcon Hurst—Journal of Modern Literature. October, 1970.
Bone, David—Memories of Conrad—The Saturday Review of Literature, 7 November 1925.
Clifford, Hugh—Joseph Conrad: Some Scattered Memories; The Bookman's journal and print Collector No, 10, 1924.
Conrad Ford and the Sources of Chance Conradiane a Vol. VII, 1976.
Couch Tour of Joseph Conrad's Home in Kent, Joseph Conrad Society Pamphlet, 1974.
Davis, Harold E.—Conrad's Revision of The Secret Agent: A study in Literary impression; Modern language Quarterly Sept, 1958.
De, Terrant Andzew—An Unknown Episode of Conrad's Life, New Statement and Nation, 28 July, 1988.

Dougles, Robin—My Boyhood with Conrad, Cornwill Magazine, 1929.

Dowson, Earnest—Some Recollections of Joseph Conrad; The Fortnightly Review, 1 Aug, 1928.

Dugh, Edmund—Joseph Conrad As I Knew Him, T. P's and Cassell's Weekly. 23 August, 1924.

Ellmann, Richard and Fieldson, Charless, Jr. (eds.)—The Modern Tradition. New York, Oxford University press, 1965.

Fernando, Lioyd—Conrad's Eastern Expatriates: A New Version of His Outcast. PMLA, Vol. XCI, 1976.

Folerence, Hardy—The Early Life of Thomas Hardy, New York, 1928.

Garnett, David—The Golden Echo, London, 1935.

Gettman, Royal A.—George Gissing and H.G. Wells. Their Friendship and Correspondance; London, 1961.

Gillon, Adam—The Eternal Solitary, New York Bookman Associates, 1960.

Glassman, Peter J.—Language and Being: Joseph Conrad and the Literature of personality; New York and London, Columbia University press 1976.

Hemitt, Douglas—Conrad, 1952.

Hynes Samuel—The Edwardian Turn of Mind, NJ: Princeton University press, 1968.

James, Henry—Essay in Notes on Novelists. 1914.

John, Galsworthy—Joseph Conrad: A Disquisition, Fortnightly Review, 1 April. 1908.

Karl, Fredrick R.—The significance of the Revisions in the Early Versions of Nostromo, Modern Fiction Studies, Summer, 1959.

Kirschner Paul—Conrad: The Psychologist Artist, Edinburgh, 1968.

Langbeum, Robert—The Poetry of Experience, N. Y. Norton, 1963, Oxing. Ed. 1957.

Langer, Suanne K.—Feeling and Form; New York Charles Scribners, 1963.

Leavis, F.R.—The Great Tradition, 1949.

Leing, R.D.—The Divided Self—An Existential Study in Sanity and madness, Baltimore, Penguine Books, 1965.

Lester John A. Jr.—Journey Through Despair, 1880-1914, Transformations in British Library Culture, Princeton N. J. Princeton University press, 1968.

Lewis, Johns—Conrad in 1914; The polish Review, Nos, 2 & 3, 1957.

Lijtken Otto—Joseph Conrad in the Congo. The London Mercury Vol. 5, 1930.

Marz, Lovis L.—The poetry of meditation, 2nd edn., New Haven Conn. Yale University press, 1963.

Milosz, Czeslaw—Joseph Conrad in polish Eve, In Atlantic Monthly C.C. No. 5, 1957.

Modern British Fiction (Essays in Criticism), Edited by Mark Shorer.

Palffy, Eleanor—Drunk of Conrad, The Fortnightly Review October, 1929.

Poets of Reality, Six. Twentieth Century Writers, Cambridge Mass, Harvard University press 1963.

Putnam, George P.—Conrad in Crawcow, Outlook, 3 March, 1920.

Return to Yesterday.—London, 1931.

Reynolds, Stephen—Joseph Conrad and Sea Fiction, The Quarterly Review July 1912.

Scholes, Robert and Kellogg, Robert—The Nature of Narrative, London, Oxford University press. 1966.

Story and idea in Conrad's.—The Shadow Line—Critical Quarterly Vol. II summer 1960.

Taylor, A.J.P.—English History, 1914-1945, Oxford, 1965.

The Flowers of the Forest, London, 1955.

The History of Mr. Conrad's Books.—Times Literary Supplement, 30 August, 1923.

The Modern Spirit—Essays on the Continuity of Nineteenth and Twentieth Century Literature, New York: Oxford University press, 1968.

The Rescuer Manuscript, A Key to Conrad's Development and Decline, Harvard Library Bulletin Vol. X, 1956.

Tindall, W.Y.—Apology for Marlow on R. C. Rathburn and M. Steinmann Jr. (es). From Jane Austen to Joseph Conrad (Ninneapolis: University of Minnesota press, 1959).

Title, Walter—Portraits in pencil and pen, III Joseph Conrad, The Strand Magazine June, 1924.

Van Shent, Dorothy—The English Novel: Form and Ficition; New York—Harper Torch Books, 1961 (orig. ed. 1953).

Visiak, E. H.—The Mirror of Conrad, 1955.

Warner, Oliver—Joseph Conrad, 1952.

Watt, Ian—Conrad, James and Chance. In imagined World: Essays on Some English Novels and Novelists in Honour of John Butt, Edited by Maynard Mack and Ian Gregor, London, 1968.

Watt, Ian—Conrad. James and Chance in Maynard Mack and. Ian Gregor (eds.), Imetine Worlds Essays in Honour of John Butt, London, Methsun, 1968.

Watt, Ian-Conrad—The Secret Agent, A Case Book, London, 1973.

West, Herbert Faukner, Josenh Conrad's Funeral, Saturday Review of Literature, 6 September, 1924.

Woolf, Virginia—The Common Reader, Copy Right 1925, by Harcoutt Brace and World Inc. Renewed 1953 by Leonard Woolf.

Worth, G.J.—Conrad's Debt to Maupassant in the preface to the Nigger of the Narcissus, the Journal of English and Germanic Philology No. 4, 1955.

Wright, Elizabeth Cox.—The Defining Function of Vocabulary in Conrad's—The Rover South Atlantic Quarterly Vol. 1 Lix, Spring 1960.